ADVANCE PRAISE FOR

Spirituality, Action, & Pedagogy

"This book is filled with wonderful phenomenological descriptions of holistic education in action. It is an inspirational gathering of stories and reflections demonstrating what is possible in our relationships with our students and each other when we reclaim the spiritual dimension of teaching and learning. The authors challenge us to engage with our students as whole human beings, allowing them and ourselves to live deeply into experiences of love and faith, feeling and spontaneity, self-awareness and community."

Ron Miller, Author of Caring for New Life: Essays on Holistic Education

"*Spirituality, Action, & Pedagogy: Teaching from the Heart* attempts to overcome, as one author names it, the 'poverty of abstraction and disconnection' that has dulled and distanced so much of contemporary schooling, especially higher education. The antidote, as presented in these thirteen short chapters, returns the human heart and soul to the curriculum. Each chapter from these university faculty members leads with often touching, personal accounts of teaching and living that generally form the story line for down-to-earth insights as to how we might nourish classrooms and students that are uncontracted, courageous, vulnerable, and awake in the midst of life and learning. This is an intimate, hopeful, and thoughtful collection that is rich with nuance. It will be a service to any teacher who longs for the day when education becomes a wisdom tradition."

Tobin Hart, Professor of Psychology, State University of West Georgia;
Author of The Secret Spiritual World of Children *and* From Information to
Transformation: Education for the Evolution of Consciousness

Spirituality, Action, & Pedagogy

STUDIES IN
EDUCATION
& SPIRITUALITY

Peter Laurence and Victor Kazanjian
General Editors

Vol. 8

PETER LANG
New York • Washington, D.C./Baltimore • Bern
Frankfurt am Main • Berlin • Brussels • Vienna • Oxford

Spirituality, Action, & Pedagogy

TEACHING FROM THE HEART

EDITED BY

Diana Denton
& Will Ashton

PETER LANG
New York • Washington, D.C./Baltimore • Bern
Frankfurt am Main • Berlin • Brussels • Vienna • Oxford

Library of Congress Cataloging-in-Publication Data

Spirituality, action, & pedagogy: teaching from the heart /
edited by Diana Denton, Will Ashton.
p. cm. — (Studies in education and spirituality; v. 8)
Includes bibliographical references.
1. Reflective teaching. 2. Spirituality. I. Denton, Diana.
II. Ashton, Will. III. Series.
LB1027.3.S65   371.102—dc22   2003022527
ISBN 0-8204-7061-9
ISSN 1527-8247

Bibliographic information published by **Die Deutsche Bibliothek**.
Die Deutsche Bibliothek lists this publication in the "Deutsche
Nationalbibliografie"; detailed bibliographic data is available
on the Internet at http://dnb.ddb.de/.

Cover design by Joni Holst

The paper in this book meets the guidelines for permanence and durability
of the Committee on Production Guidelines for Book Longevity
of the Council of Library Resources.

Printed in the United States of America

Contents

PART TWO
TRANSFORMING PRACTICES

PART THREE
EMBODYING POETICS

Acknowledgments

This book originated from a panel presentation at the 2002 National Communication Association Convention. We are indebted to all the participants who stirred our reflections and practice. We would also like to thank the many students who have inspired our journeys as teachers and helped us to restore the heart to teaching.

We would like to express our gratitude to the Spirituality and Education series co-editor, Peter Laurence for his insightful editorial assistance. He provided valuable encouragement for this book from its first inception. We also extend our appreciation to those at Peter Lang Publishing for their assistance. We would first like to thank Heidi Burns who guided the book through the editorial process and completed the copyediting of the manuscript. Sophie Appel, Production Manager and Lisa Dillon, Production and Creative Director facilitated the production process with care and attention.

We would also like to express our gratitude to the Department of Drama and Speech Communication at the University of Waterloo for its support of this project.

Excerpt from *The Essential Rumi* (1995). (Coleman Barks, trans.). New York: HarperSanFrancisco. Used by permission of Coleman Barks.

Excerpt from *Jewish Stories One Generation Tells Another* (1987/1996). Schram, P. Northvale, NJ: Jason Aronson. Reprinted by permission of the publisher. All rights reserved.

Excerpt from KOL HANESHAMAH (1994), Shapiro, R. M. Phil: The Reconstructionist Press. Reprinted by permission of the publisher.

DIANA DENTON AND WILL ASHTON

Introduction

Teaching from the Heart

The idea for this project was born from a conference panel that asked participants to consider whether or not our schools and our classrooms were places where our hearts were nourished and developed along with our minds. The panelists were invited to come together and share stories of how they had experienced an awakening of the heart in their teaching, as well as to pose additional questions concerning how matters of the spirit fit into our educational lives. The response from panelists and audience alike generated the idea of collecting additional stories of "teaching from the heart" that were grounded in immediate teaching experience and practice.

This book extends an invitation to the reader to take part in a personal exploration of what it means to consciously seek the heart of education. Something delightfully contagious emerged from that initial dialogue, resulting in this effort at widening the conversation. Here is a collection of committed voices addressing what is surely one of the most provocative questions that confronts any of us who have stood at the front of a classroom. Whether we are in K-12 or higher education the central problem of our professional existence is "Why do we teach?" This can be a very tricky question and of course there are no easy answers. Part of the problem is that when we ask ourselves why we teach we are inviting a manifold of possibilities into our consciousness. We are in fact opening a door to a labyrinth, exposing ourselves to uncertainty, ambiguity, and doubt. The authors in this collection respond to the challenge by striking the most personal chords of lived experience. They relate their tales of spirituality and teaching in such a way that the reader will be coaxed into confronting his or her own understanding of what it means to teach.

Not surprisingly we find that embedded in the question of why we teach is the even more profound problem of what education is and should be. John Dewey understood education as a collective enterprise through which we actively create our world. Paulo Freire, whose writings on oppression and education inspired the critical pedagogy movement, also saw teaching and learning as essentially a world-creating process. Dewey and Freire both recognized that teaching is a communal enterprise of shared meaning between free agents in immediate personal contexts. The reader will find in these stories personal narratives that collectively build a case for why we must never lose sight of the moral and spiritual foundations of the educational enterprise, an enterprise that self-consciously recognizes itself as world-creating activity. One of our goals is to recover the educative value of ordinary lived experience, the revelations often contained in moments of emergent practice in actual classrooms.

Each of these narratives demonstrates the power of spiritually reflective teaching to help insure that these questions remain consciously and actively at the center of all we do as teachers and educators. It is our hope that these stories will inspire others to work toward clarifying and shifting the balance away from educational processes that privilege hierarchy, competition, and material self-gratification, and toward authentic engagements honoring love, community, and justice. Our ambitions are not modest because we believe in the work teachers can do to bring the heart back into our lives and into the lives of students.

In his book, *Moral Outrage in Education,* David Purpel (1999) observes "perhaps we ought to conduct our lives as if our history were to be read by our great-grandchildren as they seek to find wisdom and inspiration in the past" (p. 180). Purpel calls on us to craft our individual journeys as a map for future travelers. The teachers writing in this book have already embarked on this path. Some are far along and others are just starting out. We've tried to include diverse voices in this collection. The reader will find an array of multicultural perspectives that also reflect a wide range of life experience, teaching contexts, and theoretical/philosophical orientations, but the diversity of narrative styles and distinctive voices all join in unfolding stories of presence, transformation, and practice.

We believe the reader will experience some of the joy, inspiration, and excitement that we shared as the project came together. We could not have known in advance the depth of feeling and emotion these stories would generate, and we are encouraged that the results bear direct testimony to the power of language and communication to transform. We invite readers to open their hearts to the multiplicity of wisdom and nascent understanding these stories evoke. We find that each of these tales constitutes part of a larger whole. Our own reading of the chapters reveals that collectively the project constitutes a phenomenology of *teaching from the heart*.

We have decided to organize the book around three recurring themes: "Positioning Spirituality," "Transforming Practices," and "Embodying Poetics." Because such categorizing seems rooted in a logic too linear to do justice to the multiplicity that each chapter embodies, we invite readers to engage their own logics as they move from part to whole and back again. Each of the chapters represents a center relative to all the others, and the reader moves within a circle of shared insight and experience. Connections are possible between elements everywhere, from practices of traditional medicine in Mexico to concepts of the heart in the spiritual philosophy of the East. The metaphor of organization is not a hierarchy of the mind but a radiating center of the heart, and always, the emphasis is on embodied experience and practice in the classroom.

The first papers in this book focus on how we position spirituality in our educational practice, how we find and clear space for spirit in our work. Through story and experience, Arduini offers insight into this intentional positioning of spirituality in the world of the classroom. He examines the presence of spirituality in education in terms of an interrelated trilogy of individual spirit, transcendent spirit, and religious spirit and outlines four lessons that show how spirit can be more fully experienced in the classroom by avoiding dogma, emphasizing student narratives, teaching explicitly spiritual texts, and bearing witness through personal disclosure. Warren and Fassett wonder how to negotiate within and around the boundaries of identity, sexuality, and spirituality as they move towards an engaged pedagogy of mind, body, and spirit. They explore the cultivation of a teaching persona that embraces dualities, binaries, and seeming polar opposites. Hostetter calls for "communities of spirit" that are intellectually, spiritually, and socially engaged to sustain us and that enable us to learn with others. As we learn to co-create our own stories and pursue justice and compassion for others, we also learn to teach (and live) out of love instead of fear. Finally, Toll examines teacher change from a Buddhist perspective. Reflecting on notions of impermanence, nonattachment, and compassion, she describes her own success at reframing the concept of "teacher change," the process of changing and being changed in the institutional and personal environments of education.

Several chapters in this book focus on practices that are transforming. Some of these are classroom practices while others are practices and learning strategies extending beyond but also returning to the classroom. Ashton's description of his ten-year apprenticeship with Master Suh In Hyuk, an Asian martial art teacher and healer, forms a backdrop for reflections on how the metaphor of "love flows" is enacted in classroom practice. He tells the tale of how he was inspired to discover the wisdom concealed in the enigmatic advice of his teacher and how that advice became active and alive in the very different environment of a university teacher preparation program. Schmeeckle explores the embodiment of spiritual presence in the classroom as she integrates personal meditative practice and a passion for life that leaks into her teaching. Viewing students as holistic human beings, and connecting teaching to a sense of life-purpose, she describes how the spirit helps her to shape a new role as an assistant professor of sociology at a large university. Schram encourages educators and learners to tell stories in and out of the classroom, as she engages storytelling as heartfelt practice through an exploration of the Jewish tradition of storytelling. Drawing upon her own experience as a child listening to her father weep as he sang prayers in the synagogue, Schram connects spirituality and storytelling to the wisdom tradition depicted in the Torah and describes how the art of storytelling can awaken the spirit in all of us. She reminds us of stories that touch the heart. Hoth attends to the spirit of place as the ground of an engaged and courageous pedagogy, a concentration on connections between self and environment that require willing submission to "the local and ordinary" as the beginning of wisdom. Houston invites students to connect with the "spirit of the real" in his discussion of pedagogical practices that extend beyond the classroom walls. Exploring his work with students in site-specific theatre, he embarks on a journey of interrelation with site and other that opens us to the wonder of the real. He encourages students to bring their "dreams" into the light of day. In the real spaces of experience we touch the unknown, the unpredictable, the mysteries of spirit.

In the final section of this collection, the chapters focus on an embodied poetics. Menchaca draws on Mexican spiritual traditions as she considers the state of fright known as *susto,* a state of shock that throws the soul out of the body, and the healing role of the teacher as *curandera,* whose role is to lovingly and compassionately call back connection and responsibility. Through a poetic rendering of the world, Snowber welcomes the detours of our lives as a place to migrate to the heart of body and soul. She asks how we can lean into the uninvited guests of our lives, whether these are people, experiences, illnesses, broken plans, or the delight and limitation of our bodies. Through the spiritual practice of walking, she is invited into a deeper intimacy with the natural world, which becomes a teacher to her. She explores how we can reframe our lives, reshaping our ways of seeing and finding a way to tend the earth through tending the flesh of our spirits. Denton explores the embodiment of images of the heart as she reflects on the tantric conception of spiritual liberation as to become something that moves in the heart. She considers the role of the teacher as a source of inspiration and presence to awaken this movement of the heart in students whose experience of education has excluded all but the detached mind in the idea of learning. Poulos engages in an unmasking of the heart through teaching the Other. This encounter with an Other is explored as the ignition of a holy, limitless light—a light that calls us out into the open, lays us bare, burns in us, and opens us to possibility. In heartful, spirited education, we are filled with questions. The author offers a story of risk and gift, of teaching and learning as acts of courage, of dreaming in the dark and dancing in the light.

The papers in this book offer a re-visioning of education. In a political and economic environment driven by the allure of "accountability," "externally imposed standards," and "outcome-based assessment," it seems increasingly difficult to find support for a pedagogical practice that self-consciously engages spirit along with mind. It is easy for teachers to lose heart. The contributors to this volume represent a new wave of resistance to institutional hierarchy and dogma. The authors, we think, are teachers who are willing to risk their hearts in the classroom. More than technique, they bring heart, body, and soul to their students, the integrity of presence. In their stories they acknowledge the messiness, uncertainties, wonders, and richness of this practice. Their writing is invitational. If we as educators, readers and authors alike, are to be released from institutional constraint, we must have the courage to recover a "heartfelt" practice that returns a unity of body, mind, and spirit to the classroom—one that enlivens and welcomes all who enter the halls of learning. We invite the reader to join us as we engage the world creating activity of teaching from the heart.

Reference

Purpel, D. (1999). *Moral outrage in education.* New York: Peter Lang.

PART I

POSITIONING SPIRITUALITY

The Songbird in the Superstore

How the Spirit Enters the Classroom

In the past, my concerns as a teacher became largely bound up in measuring the observable behaviors of my students. I felt that these behaviors served as evidence of learning, which is the goal of education after all. By focusing on clear behaviors, I was getting away from what I considered to be the capriciousness of instructors I had known as a student. These instructors seemed to grade based on how well a student spoke in class, if a student agreed with them, or some other, hidden, criteria.

This "objective" approach has its disadvantages, not the least of which is its impersonal nature. It makes students, as whole persons, peripheral to measuring what they accomplish. Students' lives, beyond the specific evidence of their learning, had become background to me. As a result, one valuable resource, their spiritual lives, had become ignored or proscribed or at least irrelevant, considered by me as too personal or separate from education.

In addition to this lack of the personal and the spiritual, higher education in general is concerned more with knowledge than with wisdom. This argument stands to reason in a postmodern world where meaning is widely contested. However, this lack of clear connection with a deeper meaning had created a void in my experience as a teacher. My teaching was uncertain, ready to be contradicted by the next survey that tells what was wrong with what we teachers believed last week. This attitude is partly due to a consumer mentality in which all things, including knowledge, become commodities. Knowledge must be constantly updated and refined to produce better, more valuable products for the student/consumer to purchase.

Spayde (1998), in discussing a variety of modes of education, characterizes the liberal arts as "slow knowledge," which is built up over a long time in comparison to fast knowledge, which changes rapidly. However, in teaching liberal arts, specifically speech communication, I find the opposite to be true. I see a rapid consumption of knowledge occurring as students and teachers feel the need to keep up with the latest literature available. Spirituality, in the form of religious traditions, is the ultimate in slow knowledge, as these teachings are tested over centuries.

Schwehn (1993) explains the impersonal nature of the academy as the result of a historic model of the researcher originally formulated by Max Weber. Schwehn critiques Weber's model as ascetic because the academy loses the values gained from religion, that are replaced with knowledge-making values. He states that academics renounced "spontaneous enjoyment, emotional satisfaction, and communal affections . . . without the religious consolations, assurances, and commitments that might have made sense of such self-abnegating behavior" (p. 14). The academician, then, has the worst of both worlds—ascetic rigor without the comfort of spiritual rewards. Much of this description fits my experience as a college teacher. Students and teachers routinely sacrifice time, energy, and community, and are rewarded with the amorphous values of teaching and learning concepts and skills within a prescribed curriculum.

My experience of the spiritual in education is limited, yet there have been times when the spirit has entered my classroom. It has happened, not as a planned experience, but because the liveliness of classroom interaction permitted it to enter unbidden. I compare spirituality to the birds that enter "mega" stores, not as a planned aspect of these warehouse-like commercial buildings, but because the stores cannot exclude all of the elements of the environment within which they exist. The classroom, likewise, creates an environment within a wider social context. The boundaries of these environments are necessarily permeable.

This image of the unbidden entering the educational environment has positive and negative aspects. While education tends to focus on developing the intellectual lives of students and teachers, this narrow view can ignore important aspects of the people engaged in teaching and learning. On the other hand, spiritual ideas may seem inappropriate or irrelevant in a public education that separates religion and government. Additionally, the spiritual nature of students and teachers may be subject to interrogation and contestation, which certainly could create an irrelevant distraction from the process of education. On the other hand, such agonistic pursuits could lead to deeper and more meaningful kinds of learning. Despite the potential drawbacks, I am drawn to the spiritual as a possible remedy for the emptiness that I feel when I limit my teaching to the coldness of a strictly objective approach.

In the following I describe my understanding of spirituality as it relates to pedagogy, my experiences of spirituality in the classroom, and, finally, I offer some suggestions on how to move positively toward the conscious practice of allowing spirit to enter into one's teaching.

Defining Terms

To remedy the emptiness that seems to condition so much in education today, I have developed three categories of spirituality and pedagogy. This list is certainly not exhaustive, but it highlights some important aspects of spirituality. These are based on my reflection on spirituality in general, a review of the literature, and my experience with spirituality in the classroom. The first two ways of looking at spirit encompass two poles of the same idea: individual spirit and transcendence. The third, religious tradition, refers to the specific practices, values, and knowledge associated with a given faith.

First, some writers define spirit in terms of the individual's spirit, which may be seen as one's self or one's soul. The spirit in this sort of understanding is the "true" self that one must learn about and, ideally, operate from (Fenwick, English, and Parsons, 2000). The concern of practices based on this view is the maximization of the individual's potential. Nash (2001) states that, for some people, ". . . spirituality, more than religion, emphasizes the vital principle or animating force within all living beings, the 'breath of life' that is incorporeal, the force that makes us truly who we are" (p. 25). This voice that enters the classroom is the songbird of the self. The unique power of the individual is often directly suppressed in a classroom setting much of the time as the focus is on the classroom as a group.

A second way that I would define spirituality is that it provides a context for any person as part of a much larger reality. We may call this larger entity the "life-force," or God, or some other designation. The primary characteristic here is the recognition that something transcends the individual experience and gives meaning to experience. Berger (1969) suggests the importance of this experience of transcendence and lays out specific "signals of transcendence." He states that

> . . . human life gains the greatest part of its richness from the capacity for ecstasy, by which I do not mean the alleged experiences of the mystic, but any experience of stepping outside the taken-for-granted reality of everyday life, any openness to the mystery that surrounds us on all sides. (p. 75)

Berger offers several of these "signals of transcendence" as evidence that the supernatural operates in human experience universally in the forms of order, play, hope, damnation, and humor. For Berger, each of these is essential, and each also points to a reality beyond empirical testing.

This aspect of the spirit that must enter the classroom, whether intended or not, is the songbird of the world. These are moments when we recognize common characteristics that enable the individuals in the room to participate in a larger human experience, whether it be the shock of death or the joy of play and creation.

A third orientation that is often labeled as spiritual is the invocation of specific religious traditions. Schwehn (1993), using a particular tradition as an example, argues that American higher education and Christian practices are intimately related. Speaking primarily of education from the teacher's point of view, Schwehn argues that academicians are primarily concerned with making knowledge, leaving little room for community and values that are Christian. Speaking of Weber's model of the academic, he states:

> But on Weber's account, the process of knowledge formation, if conducted rationally, really does favor and cultivate the emergence of a particular personality type. And this personality does exhibit virtues—clarity, but not charity; honesty, but not friendliness; devotion to calling, but not loyalty to particular and local communities of learning. (p. 18)

Schwehn's critique of academic values comes from his religious tradition, and he argues that this specific tradition is necessary, saying, "one cannot be 'religious in general,' but that one must speak . . . from a particular religious tradition" (p. 136).

This dimension of spirituality I will call the songbird of the Way. In the process of worshipping, celebrating, and analyzing forces greater than human life, religious traditions have created powerful works of art and thought. To the extent that those who enter the classroom and society have been influenced by religious tradition, this, too, is a voice that will be present.

Each of these three spiritual orientations offers an opportunity for individuals to include more of themselves in educational practices. Each also has various hazards related to it, not the least of which is the potential for oppression of other beliefs, especially if the teacher initiates practices that promote a specific spiritual orientation. Because of this, care is needed when inviting the spirit to enter into the classroom. I believe that there must always be room for affirmation of spirit, but also students in particular must be given space for their own, possibly contradictory, orientations.

Recognizing Spirit in Moments of Storytelling

Reflection on the absence of spirituality in my teaching causes me to think about those moments when, unbidden, spirituality has entered my classroom. What follows is a description of these events and the generalizations I can make about such experiences as they relate to the three notions of spirit outlined above. The final section discusses how such experiences point to practices that allow the spirit to come forth in one's teaching.

These experiences are stories of peak moments in my teaching, quite unintended by me. Perhaps I facilitated these moments through openness to what students and I have to offer, but, as is often the case, spontaneous events triggered unique teachable moments. These moments vary in who and what is being taught, but they have in common two qualities: First, they are moments when I felt a unique connection with both the subject matter and with my students; and second, they all happen to be moments of storytelling. This second quality is significant in terms of methods that may facilitate the entrance of spirit into education. These specific events are unique moments in my life as a teacher, and I respectfully retell them, knowing they are not just my stories but stories I hold in common with my students over the course of twenty years.

The Songbird of the Self in Appalachia

The first definition of spirit I offered above is the expression of self. While teaching in Eastern Kentucky, I was honored to teach a unique student population. Characteristic of this particular culture is their awareness of a strong negative stereotype and a negative self-image as a result. This stereotype is perpetuated in the word "hillbilly," and it is generally imposed from outside the region and outside the social group to which it refers. This negative image is in sharp contrast to a pride in tradition and pride in resourcefulness that most Appalachians possess, since the history of this group is characterized by an ongoing fight against many natural and human obstacles.

I was teaching an "off-campus" class for Hazard Community College in 1990. This night class was held in a high school classroom in a nearby town. While teaching communication courses I often use word games to demonstrate problems in understanding that are due to the nature of communication and language. In response to various language "puzzles," a student mentioned a joke he knew that was similar. I asked him to write it on the board, and this is what he wrote:

M R puppies.
M R not puppies.
M R puppies 2.
M R not puppies.
M R puppies. C M P N?

Perhaps this is not a joke unique to the region, but I was not familiar with it. I laughed and made sure to write it down to share with my wife later. The rest of the students laughed or groaned, recognizing a well-worn double-edged joke. While it was a joke that involved dialect and seemed self-effacing, it also expressed the student's identity, his self-awareness, and his sense of humor. Later that semester the same student shared other aspects of his identity as an Appalachian when he brought in pawpaw, the fruit of a tree that had grown wild through most of the middle of the United States but has now become rare.

This student's willingness to share his identity with an outsider was a risky move. He was brave to get up in front of class and tell a joke that had considerable ambiguity. His fellow students could have interpreted the joke as a criticism of their dialect when told in the presence of an outsider.

Conversely, it could be perceived as a moment where I was treated as an insider, who could understand this joke about dialect. This was one of my first lessons in living in Eastern Kentucky, which to me was a region filled with contradictions. This student exhibited a pride that I did not always see, as students were well aware of negative stereotypes about Appalachians.

By handing him the chalk in that moment I opened up an opportunity for the student to be the center of the class, and I think this encouraged the student to continue to reveal himself and his knowledge of his heritage. Many students I taught really desired to separate themselves from "old-fashioned" ways.

As unremarkable as it is, handing him the chalk was a small act of faith that what he had to say was worth hearing. It paid off for me, as I gained an enthusiastic expert on a region that still seemed foreign to me. The songbird of the spirit is here in that this student revealed a side of himself that he may not have expressed otherwise. Through this experience, he and perhaps others who were ambivalent about their identity as Appalachians discovered a source of power in their selfhood.

The Songbird of the World: Tutoring in the Indochinese Project

Around 1980, the Indochinese migration created challenges for many communities as they worked to integrate these refugees into U.S. society. Many were non-literate, causing great difficulty in learning the survival English they needed in the United States. I was hired to tutor some of them at Sauk Valley Community College in the small town of Dixon, Illinois. I was only a few years out of high school at this point, and this was my first teaching experience.

Because I was one of the least experienced of the teachers, I was given a relatively advanced group to work with. Still, the challenge of simply communicating with them was quite daunting. My students, mostly men who had been subsistence farmers in the hills of Laos, were very respectful of me as a teacher, and we had some successes. Even so I knew a great deal of misunderstanding limited our communication and learning. One day as I was wracking my brain for material they could use for reading, I remembered that I had enjoyed Aesop's Fables as a child and I thought that perhaps these adult second-language learners might enjoy them, too. I felt that the brevity of these stories would make them easy to read and that the students would enjoy them because they had broad moral themes.

When we began reading the fables, one of my more advanced students said that they had similar stories in their country. What followed was one of our more active meetings, with my students finally having some material that they could draw on to practice English. We finally had a common experience to talk about, and they also attempted to tell stories they knew well as I listened.

As we exchanged stories, there seemed to be a different tone in how we spoke to each other. Prior to this, limited vocabularies held up our communication, but also having no common frame of reference limited our understanding. Suddenly, we had a rather large body of information to talk about and to compare. Do you know about the story of the sour grapes? You know about the lion with the thorn in its paw? Oh, but it is a tiger in your story.

This fairly simple connection, quite unplanned, demonstrates to me that spirit is a border crosser, a transgressor of linguistic and cultural boundaries. This example could be explained in a number of ways. I know, for instance, that many of the Vietnamese and Laotions I taught had interacted with the French in their homeland, so perhaps they had heard Aesop's Fables through them. However, I am inclined to believe these stories were folk tales that demonstrate that we can find commonality and transcendence through storytelling.

In any case, the voice of age-old storytellers, the songbirds of the world, showed me that these students had enjoyed the same stories and the same literary genre of the fable. For them, I think this experience reassured them that the place to which they had escaped was not utterly alien.

The Songbird of the Way: Sharing Religious Ideas versus Evangelization

While teaching a course on small group communication at Southern Illinois University in Carbondale, Illinois, I was searching for an exercise that would give my class a format for modeling group leadership. I was a graduate teaching assistant, and I had never taught this particular topic. I did not have a lot of material to draw from. Despite having a good instructor's manual and helpful materials from several colleagues, I was stumped. As I sat staring at my bookshelf I noticed *Zen Flesh, Zen Bones*, compiled by Paul Reps. I remembered that it contained several *koans*, brief stories used in Zen Buddhism to train adherents on the path toward enlightenment. To my surprise I was able to fashion an engaging exercise in group decision-making from this material. The open and highly ambiguous nature of the material worked well, as the stories' meanings could be debated readily. Here is an example of one of the *koans* I used:

> "Our schoolmaster used to take a nap every afternoon," related a disciple of Soyen Shaku. "We children asked him why he did it and he told us: 'I go to dreamland to meet the old sages just as Confucius did.'" When Confucius slept, he would dream of ancient sages and later tell his followers about them.
>
> "It was extremely hot one day so some of us took a nap. Our schoolmaster scolded us. 'We went to dreamland to meet the ancient sages the same as Confucius did,' we explained. 'What was the message from those sages?' our schoolmaster demanded. One of us replied: 'We went to dreamland and met the sages and asked them if our schoolmaster came there every afternoon, but they said they had never seen any such fellow.'" (p. 38)

These stories are useful, not only for communication training but for allowing spirit to enter into the classroom. As the class started working on the assignment, the students were confused about how to decide on a meaning for the story they were given because many stories have self-evident meanings. As they discussed them, the multiplicity of meanings became clearer and the task became harder. Does the story mean that diverse perceptions of reality are equal? Does it call authority into question? Is it just a funny story about someone caught in a lie? While I briefly explained the nature of the stories, I did not explain the belief system in any detail. Still, I think students appreciated that these stories had a complexity, which was not apparent at first sight. It gave them a bit of experience with a different belief system. Students gained some knowledge of a belief system that did not give ready answers and commandments. The voice of the songbird of the Way was, in this case, a fairly intellectual voice that called students to question meanings and perception.

Implications: Toward a More Intentional Practice

I would derive three lessons from this reflection. The first and most important lesson is that the spiritual dimension needs to be offered as a particular and personal insight, rather than a final, objective fact. This avoids the problem of dogmatism.

Nash (2001) is instructive about religious discussions, and these guidelines apply to spirituality in education generally. First, concerning religious traditions, he states that religion can be discussed in state-supported schools, though state supported schools must not "favor" a particular religion. He suggests the following approach as needed in discussing religion:

> It is my position that, particularly in the academy, religion must find an educationally appropriate voice. This is not a voice that panders, promotes, proselytizes, or practices. Rather, it is a voice that students must explore openly for its narrative strength and weaknesses, just as they have with any other kind of "voice" in the curriculum. (p. 5)

Nash's recognition of a variety of voices is important for a reflective practice of sharing spirituality in education. Many societal voices enter the classroom, and each needs to be recognized. This dialogic and multi-voiced education is another way of saying that classrooms are nested environments of social interaction. Spirituality is a vitally important voice (or songbird), as I have tried to identify through the examples above.

The second lesson I derive from this reflection is that the narrative mode seems to be an effective vehicle for allowing spirit to enter the classroom. If we are concerned with sharing specific religious traditions, for example, the narrative has two advantages. First, a story may be offered for just what it is—a story. The Zen Buddhist *koan* can be seen within the religious tradition as a means of advancing toward enlightenment. It can also be viewed as a curiously rich story. Second, the richness of a religious tradition can be retained in story form while the ultimate meaning of the story remains open to discussion and interpretation.

Third, spirit is a place where students and teachers can find connection. Conventional roles that define classroom interactions can be transcended when spirit enters the classroom. Whether we describe this quality as teacher immediacy (McCroskey et al., 1995) or as "an act of love" (Freire, 1997), spirit does constitute a resource for connection that must be allowed to enter into our educational lives.

Finally, I would like to come full-circle back to my initial observation about my own teaching. It seems to me that teaching and learning occur in a dialectic that runs between the personal and the impersonal. To teach requires intimacy and knowledge, proximity and distance, connection and objectivity. This tension, in my view, never gets fully resolved, but what is clear is that many aspects of personality can be disclosed, and discussing a person's spirituality should be no different from discussing one's age, hobbies, family life, and so on.

Summary

Spirit enters our classrooms whether we recognize it or not. It is a source of wisdom that has great potential to transform our educational environments into ones that are more open and caring, and that will be capable of sustaining us in the challenging days ahead. While not always a conscious choice, spirituality has entered my classroom and transformed it. I have seen spirit take form as

- individual expression of one's unique humanity;
- the recognition of transcendence;
- the expression of religious traditions.

As I work toward developing my teaching into a more intentional practice I focus attention on four areas. First, spirituality needs to be seen as a one of many perspectives, and surely not as something to be imposed on others. Second, spirituality somehow seems to reside in the narrative form and thus stories can be a powerful vehicle for connection and transformation. Third, some very specific curricular needs can be met through use of materials based in specific religious traditions. Lastly, the arrival or disclosure of spirit in the classroom carries with it the same value and risk as any self-disclosing for teachers and students.

I do not share Schwehn's (1993) answer to the problem of asceticism in the academy, which is to include a specific religious tradition as part of the life of higher education. However, he expresses a hope similar to mine, which is the hope that education not be an impersonal matter of knowledge creation and dissemination. Instead, my wish is that learning can be facilitated through spiritual practices and that in our learning communities we come together to share wisdom as well as knowledge.

References

Berger, P. (1969). *A rumor of angels: Modern society and the rediscovery of the supernatural.* Garden City, NY: Anchor Press.

Fenwick, T., English, L., & Parsons, J. (2001, May). *Dimensions of spirituality: A framework for adult educators*. Paper presented at the Canadian Association for the Study of Adult Education, Quebec, Canada.

Freire, P. (1997). *Pedagogy of the oppressed*. (20th anniversary ed.). New York: Continuum Press. (Original work published 1970)

McCroskey, J., et al. (1995). A cross-cultural and multi-behavioral analysis of the relationship between nonverbal immediacy and teacher evaluation. *Communication Education, 44*, 281–291.

Nash, R. J. (2001). *Religious pluralism in the academy: Opening the dialogue*. New York: Peter Lang.

Reps, P. (Ed.). (n. d.). *Zen bone, Zen flesh: A collection of Zen and pre-Zen writings*. Garden City, NY: Anchor Press.

Schwehn, M. R. (1993). *Exiles from Eden: Religion and the academic vocation in America*. Oxford, England: Oxford University Press.

Spayde, J. (1998, May–June). Learning in the key of life. *Utne Reader*, 45–49.

Spiritually Drained and Sexually Denied

Sketching an Engaged Pedagogy

We were wondering, bottom?
—A comment from John's course evaluations

Are you family?
—A common question posed to Deanna

We approach the question of spirituality cautiously. Are we spiritual? Does spirituality come into our classrooms through our teaching practices? Do we teach our students to think about issues of the spirit? As supervisors of large, multi-section introductory courses, do we ask our "young" teachers to teach in spiritual ways? What does spirituality mean to us?

We also approach the question of sexuality cautiously. As "straight-appearing," we fear response, questions, critiques about who we are, what we advocate, and the effect of our voice on this issue. However, the question of sexuality is always ever present in our minds as we enter the classroom space, a space that is never safe, never free from that question about who we are, what we do, and our collective worth. Sexuality—our performance of identity—is always at play. What does it mean to be sexual in the class-room—to be a being marked by sexuality? What does it mean to be located within heterosexual privilege, yet know this kind of simplistic have/have-not construction does not contain us? What does sexuality mean to us?

The fact that we begin this essay fearing that spirituality and sexuality are different, if not antithetical, says much about how we orient to each.

However, the assumption of such a separation leaves us intellectually and pedagogically impoverished. Too often we speak of sexual orientations as though they are fixed and immutable, something to out or to closet, to assume or deny. We treat our religions similarly, articulating spirituality as Catholic or Protestant, Taoist or Hindu, Christian or Muslim. In both instances, how we label our lives leads us to either/or alternatives, to fragments, to disconnections. We school ourselves into accepting that we are either straight or gay, pious or infidel, even when that is not how we live our lives. Compartmentalizations are easy, but they are not always truthful. Teachers, of any age and stage, face particularly untenable circumstances, largely because both sexuality and spirituality are controlled, circumscribed, and legislated. To engage sexuality in the classroom, to highlight and explore, is to invoke religious fervor. To engage spirituality, or, perhaps more properly, spiritualities, in the classroom is to invoke secular fervor. Each provides avenues to construct and deconstruct the other; the avenues emerge through the slippage between our linguistic binaries: Religion is not the same as spirituality, piety is not the same as heterosexuality, and so on.

Given these dualistic constructions—these rigid assumptions and the places where they slip and chafe against one another—how does a caring, committed educator begin? In this essay, we take such reasoned and critical explorations and transgressions to be a necessary first step. Each of us advocates a pedagogical politics of conscious ambiguity—the cultivation of a teaching persona that embraces dualities, binaries, seeming polar opposites. This is, in many ways, a trickster pedagogy, but it is not without stability, caring or concern.

Resisting and Rethinking Spirit

Our first impressions on questions of the spirit:
From Deanna:

> I suspect my thinking about "spirituality" has to do with my upbringing in what I think of as a critical-atheist household. If I came home excited about "the first Thanksgiving," my mom would tell me horror stories of smallpox–infested blankets. If I came home wanting to say grace before dinner, she would indulge me and then tell me stories of atrocities committed in the name of religion—against people of color, against gays and lesbians, against

the heretical. I grew up assuming spirit was about the Holy spirit, one vector in the Christian trinity, one aspect of a symbol of domination and destruction. No doubt this is very different from what one would learn in a home that celebrated mass and Easter and church socials.

From John:

> I was always taught to be suspicious of spirituality. When my aunt died of cancer, I remember the pastor talking about death, heaven, and the celebration of God's will. I remember thinking about how unfulfilled I felt, how sad I was that her life was reduced to dogma, to a repeated story about death. I remember my mother crying, whispering under her breath that this man, this man with a collar, never even mentioned her life, her family, and the fact that she was taken from us at such a young age. When my grandmother, my mother's mother, died two years later, my mother refused to let anyone speak about her—instead, she crafted a narrative of her life—a celebration of who my grandmother was and how she touched the lives of those around her. For her, it was a way to resist the violence she had felt from those preaching holistic practice through a lens of religious doctrine.

In many ways, one might suggest that given our own positions, we resist the incorporation of spirituality in the classroom, inasmuch as this omission means denying the assumption of Christianity—or for that matter other religions—in our classrooms. However, as we have grown as teachers, we have found and built new definitions and viewpoints. Recently, we have both begun extended dialogue and reading on the role of spirit in our classrooms, asking when the foregrounding of a more holistic enactment of self might breed a more critical and involved classroom experience for us and our students:

From Deanna:

> When I now think of spirit, I think of the interconnectedness of all life—a cosmic systems theory. We act and react, ail and heal, begin and end in tension with all things. So spirituality, for me, is about bringing a sense of interconnectedness to the world around us, to show how the classroom is a metaphor for the world, or that war is a foil for both hubris and righteous fury, or that our bodies are epistemological sites—that we learn from our bodies what is truthful and what is false (as we can never quite apprehend what is real and what is not). It is in this sense that I practice what hooks (1994) would call radical, engaged pedagogy. She notes that such a pedagogy emerges from critical and feminist thinking—work that acknowledges and celebrates difference. For hooks, such a pedagogy is performative because it calls to the forefront those things that separate and unite us: our skin colors, our body sizes/

shapes, our choices in lovers, our senses of human genesis, our fluid and frozen movements—in short, our lived experiences. Such an accounting reveals our interconnectedness, that which calls us to explore how we fit in relation to our learning. Such accoutings are revelatory and call us to become more active and vulnerable participants in our learning, whether in or outside of the classroom. hooks challenges her readers to "teach in a manner that respects and cares for the souls of our students . . . to provide the necessary conditions where learning can most deeply and intimately begin." (p. 13)

From John:

> I am drawn to hooks's (1994) notion of engaged pedagogy because I agree that teaching should include the mind, the body, and the spirit. When she argues that we are starving our students by only speaking abstractly of the mind, she is touching on a central problem in education. The body, that corporeal site of experiential knowledge, offers a theory of flesh—a way of thinking that, if tapped into, can challenge the social and political forces our students face. Moreover, hooks's articulation of spirit provides me an entry—a way of engagement that makes sense. She argues that students "want an education that is healing to the uninformed, unknowing spirit. They do want knowledge that is meaningful" (p. 19). If, in the joining of these artificially separated parts of our selves, we can foster a more meaningful educational experience, then I too would embrace the notion of spirit. Further, I would argue that asking for education to be meaningful in this way is exactly what I aim to do.

Thus, we find that what began as a suspicion of spirit was really a rejection of a certain kind of performance of spirituality—a performance of religion that does not help us, as teachers and beings in the world, articulate hope. This enactment of spirituality is less about creating a meaningful experience of our lived worlds and more about living up to another's image of how we should be. This kind of performance, this kind of reestablishment of ourselves as spiritual, leaves us wanting, empty. However, hooks (1994) opens a door to a new way of seeing—a way of being that is not about exclusion or denial of experience, but about healing, about union, about community. It is about recognizing the complicated nature of the self, appreciating the mind *with* the body and *with* the spirit.

We therefore join the conversation from the position of ambiguity—we are intrigued by spirit, but find our connection to it is, if not vague, then at least purposively messy. We are appreciative of the potential behind a new educational project that heals the ruptures and recognizes educational participants as holistic beings—an educational project that values differing life histories, differing racial/sexual/classed locations. We are excited about this project. However, we are also interested in what happens when we try to celebrate this newly articulated space in the classroom. What happens when we try to teach from the heart in ways that leave us exposed? How do we theorize (and enact that theory) from this place of vulnerability? This is the project born of this conversion toward spirituality. How does ambiguity function as a political strategy that refigures bodies, hearts, minds, and our spirits?

In the next section, we recount how we each experience our attempts to teach from our newly claimed space in the classroom—a space that challenges the mind, makes visible (and vulnerable) the body, and tries to reach the spirit of our students, even as we embrace the union in our own lived experience. For us, teaching from the heart has been most challenging when talking and teaching through sexuality. That is, what happens when the theory of teaching through the mind/body/spirit meets our sexed experiences?

John

Every semester ends in a flurry of paperwork, deadlines, grade sheets, professor evaluations, and last-minute meetings designed to make "final" decisions before the break. Last fall was one of those semesters. My desk was piled, the email inbox was full and on my phone, a tiny light stared at me in red. I was, as they say, swamped. However, comparable to most semesters, the tasks got done, the grade sheets turned in, and the evaluations conducted. This semester ended how it began—I again attempted to create a passionate, politically charged, and socially meaningful context in my classroom by having students look at mediated images of education in popular culture. I have been toying with how to turn my large, too large, 850-student lecture course into a more critical experience. It was the meeting of my theoretical and political passions with my instructional obligations. I teach in the Midwest, in what feels like a very conservative campus environment. This feeling is not as much about the Midwest, but about the specifics of my campus—a very white campus in northwestern Ohio.

In many ways, this is the perfect campus for me—a bisexual, white, middle-class, privileged man who tries to create contexts for important conversations about race, sexuality, and class. I try to make students question themselves, myself, and our interconnectedness. Lately, I have been trying to play out elements of my identity in the classroom, offering myself as a question for students. I read racially as white and middle-class—parts of my performance of self that provide less ground from which to trouble the students' assumptions of who I am. However, for many, my sexuality has always been a question mark. I appear in many contexts as straight, my female partner seemingly the only testimony one might need or desire for categorizing me. However, in my classroom (and other spaces), I purposely work toward ambiguity. That is, the performance of teacher-self I have created is one that talks openly about issues of sexuality, all the while never outing that I have a female partner nor stating my own bisexuality. I let the students read me as they desire—and they do. For many, the assumed heteronormativity of Northwest Ohio grants me the "benefit of the doubt." For others, I'm a closeted trickster, hiding "the truth" while "teasing" my students with my own queer-ness. In many ways then, I offer my body as a site for my students to question their own assumptions, their own ideas, and their own narrow-minded ideals.

As the spring semester began, I saw in my mailbox the results of my quantitative evaluations, lower than I'd like but certainly not terrible for the vastness of my course. Attached to the sheet is a sticky-note telling me all the narrative comments are behind the secretary's desk should I want to see them. Just as in every semester, I know I'll wait a few days to gain the strength to see 500+ evaluations from those who bothered to attend and, further, bothered to fill out the simple three questions asked of them. Every time I get these evaluations back I find comments about my performance of sexuality. These include the seemingly playful (with undercurrents of violence): "Warning though, his sexuality was questioned by most everyone in the class. We were wondering, bottom?" These kinds of "jokes," these insinuations of who I am are not new—they are fairly common given who I am and how I move through the world. However, the subtle violence (in the above, the image of me as the one screwed, the one seemingly lacking agency) makes the evaluations hard to read.

I pull the large binder out from behind the counter and begin flipping through—the first pass through is always about sex, always about their comments on who I am. I am intrigued (and excited) by these comments, but there, in the back of my mind, always lingers fear. About 50 pages in, under the heading "Comment on the instructor," a student has written: "Flaming." Not too bad, I think. Plus it means that the assumed heteronormativity of the class was, at the very least, disrupted. I keep flipping. About 275 pages in: "I wish the instructor would lecture naked and play with his balls while he speaks." This makes me giggle—I'm not sure how to take it, but it seems silly. At about 400 pages in, I find this: "Course sucked and the instructor was a fag!! What a flaming piece of shit." It is cliché to say that my heart stopped, but the feeling of absence, of silence, and horror as I look down at this sheet is paralyzing. I stop breathing. I'm not sure how to react. I'm immediately reminded of a lecture point I made during my language talk when I discuss Toni Morrison's Nobel Prize speech: "Oppressive language does more than represent violence; it is violence; does more than represent the limits of knowledge, it limits knowledge" (Morrison, 2000). I feel the pain, the sharpness of those comments—and I know, I know that this moment is an attack on my body, on my soul, my spirit.

I imagine going into class, trying to alter my performance, to hide and erase my presence—to be the absent professor that does not disrupt their expectations. I could, I tell myself. I could close off my body, my spirit—create an image that avoids the slings and arrows of homophobia as I lecture at them, the talking head of academic knowledge. I could do it, but would it only kill me more slowly, more quietly?

Deanna

My own "outings" in the classroom are complicated and frustrating for different reasons. Typically, I don't get any overt, institutionalized feedback on my performance of self. My institution uses those ubiquitous standardized evaluation forms, which reduce my teaching to points along a continuum from 1 to 5: 4.5, 4.4, 4.9, 4.3, and so forth. When a student engages my performance of sexuality, s/he does so subtlety, smoothly. Commonly, a student asks me if I am "family?" It took me a few times of responding, "huh?" before I finally asked a kind and outspoken student what this might mean. (This may be a characteristic of living in the San Francisco Bay Area; San Jose is 50 miles south of San Francisco, a hotbed of diverse sexualities. However, while homophobia is often more covert—perhaps more heteronormative—we've recently experienced the violent death of a transgendered youth in nearby Fremont, CA). My students assume that any overtures I make to complicate or make ambiguous my sexuality mean that I am gay—an odd correlation that assumes that only someone who is gay may have empathy for or stand in solidarity with people who demand a broader conceptualization of normal, non-deviant, celebrated sexuality. For instance, if I went on a cruise with one of my girlfriends from college, they would take this person to be a lover; if I say I have a partner, they take this to mean that I am gay (otherwise I would have said "boyfriend" or "husband"). Similarly, if I refer to my high school sweetheart or a boyfriend who loves Kerouac, then they take me to be straight. If I mix and match, reveal that many of my friends are open and exploratory about their sexuality, and take time to engage students in discussions of how communication functions to shape and mediate seemingly stable aspects of our identities, such as race, gender, and sexuality, then they don't quite know what to make of me.

Generally speaking, I feel safe in my attempts to complicate sexuality with my students. Perhaps this is because, at the end of the day, I can point to any number of assumptive instances that can "vouch" for my heterosexuality. However, most interesting to me is how my own experiences with sexuality in the classroom illustrate how heteronormativity still functions in and through me. I find myself, at the end of the day, at the beginning of the next class, at the end of the semester, wanting to say that I am, in fact, straight, to show them that though I might have an agenda, it is not the agenda they expected or assumed. Is this my attempt to construct the trickster? The person who can be relied upon to transgress for effect, to prove a point, to lay plain the tensive ties that bind us all? Alternatively, is it my attempt to claim that I have only been playing at "crooked," at complex, at queer? In either instance, this speaks to the complex choreography of classroom desires. Am I clarifying that I am straight, unthreatening, known, so that my students might one day desire me? Is it possible that I am suggesting that I am not what I appear, that I am indeed edgy, hip, radical, and transgressive, so that they might one day desire me? Perhaps I should imply that I am (un)threatening (un)known, curious, transgressive, traditional and, above all else, engaged in understanding and challenging how people, including me, are the way they are.

Educational Practice That Engages the Mind, the Body, and the Spirit

In an attempt to present selves we respect, a mode of being in the world that we feel ethically and spiritually positions us in relation to those who join our classroom communities, we find a struggle—a complicated system of hope coupled with constraint. How do we teach from the heart, teach from the position of an exposed mind, body, and spirit—a mode of engagement with our students that is honest, available, and socially just? How do we interact with (or create at least an image that might be hopeful to) our queer students, especially when we know that such enactments of self come with consequences. Bettina Heinz (2002), in a recent essay in *Communication Education,* argues that we (GLBT identified professors) should come out in the classroom, creating a discursive and material space of queerness, undermining the heteronormativity of our college class-rooms. I would suggest that to come out in this way is to teach from the juncture of the mind, body, spirit—the juncture of the political, the social, and the educational. It is to remind students that those who stand as teach-ers in our classrooms are people with lives, with histories, with complex subjectivities—to say we are people who have minds, bodies, and spirits that can be bruised and that, with this potential danger, we *still* offer our-selves to our students.

However, our essay builds from the ground forged by Heinz (2002) and others—we want to both celebrate the desire to out ourselves as one po-litically powerful strategy, while still acknowledging that such calls are, indeed, complicated (Warren & Fassett, 2002). In terms of our own iden-tities, we occupy tenuous positions, marked by ambiguity and fluidity. To be out (as bisexual, straight, or supporting), is complicated, especially when cultural codes or cues might undermine our attempts to blur iden-tities. A bisexual coupled with someone of the opposite sex occupies a contested space in conversations of sexuality; as a queer-identified person, they also enjoy the privilege of heteronormativity. How does that outing work to potentially support heteronormativity? Do homophobic students use those queer faculty as evidence—see, they can be straight if they choose to be? Thus, we end by acknowledging and recognizing the politi-cal potential of ambiguity—not necessarily the same pedagogical line we carve out here in relation to (our) sexuality in the classroom, but rather we advocate for and see hope in pushing students to see more fluid concep-tions of identity, demonstrably contested enactments of how bodies, minds, and spirits inhabit the classroom. We advocate here a celebration of multiplicity—of races, of sexes, of sexualities (and the concomitant per-formances of identities). Such flex and flux provides the performative ground from which we might create productive, subversive, and potentially liberating identity politics that might create a space for a self that unites mind, body, and spirit.

In this way, we urge teachers to recognize the interconnectedness of the mind, the body, and the spirit—to create spaces for imagining the self in different ways, to see ambiguity as a critical space for contested aspects of identity to emerge and potentially change power relationships. For the costs we surely feel in the classroom when our sense of self is opposed or challenged do not even begin to measure up to the potential that performance of self might open up for students who need the potential of that subversive space. For instance, one of the authors recently had occasion to see the potential of embracing, holistically, the mind, body, and spirit in the classroom. A young queer-identified student approached one of us and noted that s/he was appreciative of the attempt to make space for seeing his/her own self in the classroom. For this student, the attempt to create the question, read on one of our teacher-bodies, meant they could find a voice, a space to articulate their own subjectivity, their own whole self in that pedagogical space.

References

Heinz, B. (2002). Enga(y)ging the discipline: Sexual minorities and communication studies. *Communication Education, 51*, 95–104.

hooks, b. (1994). *Teaching to transgress: Education as the practice of freedom.* New York: Routledge.

Morrison, T. (2000). Nobel Lecture, 7 December 1993. In D. McQuade & R. Atwan (Eds.), *The Writer's Presence: A Pool of Readings* (3rd ed.) (pp. 762–769). Boston: Bedford/St. Martin's.

Warren, J. T., & Fassett, D. L. (2002). (Re)Constituting ethnographic identities. *Qualitative Inquiry, 8*, 575–590.

From the Heart of the Heart of Learning

A mentor of mine suggests that all of us are placed in the third grade for our whole lives, in order to learn the difference between fear and love. Among other things, one learns that fear is a shape shifter and that it appears in many forms and disguises. Learning to act out of love instead of acting out of fear has profound implications for teaching and learning. It affects what I teach, the way I teach, what I want students to learn, and how I want them to learn it. For me, learning to teach and live out of love rather than fear arises from these affirmations: First, God is love, and we are not alone; second, we must learn to co-create our own stories; third, the heart of learning includes empathy, compassion, and the pursuit of justice; and fourth, learning the love of God, self, and others is sustained by "communities of the spirit."

Recently, at my mother's funeral, I honored her for teaching me that God is love. She typically conveyed this teaching through biblical texts, such as Psalm 39:

> Where shall I go from your spirit? Or where shall I flee from your presence?
> If I ascend into heaven, you are there. . . .
> If I make my bed in hell, you are there.
> If I take the wings of the morning, and dwell in the uttermost part of the sea,
> Even there shall your hand lead me, and your right hand shall hold me.

And this passage from St. Paul:

> For I am persuaded that neither death nor life, nor angels, nor principalities,
> nor powers, nor things present, nor things to come, nor height, nor depth,

nor any other creature shall be able to separate us from the love of God. (Romans 8:38–39)

This confidence, this faith, provides a foundation, a context, for everything that I teach—for everything that I myself am attempting to learn.

In spite of the grand scale of this affirmation, a thousand faces of fear present themselves to us and to most of our students, day after day. My five-year-old daughter anticipated kindergarten for months, and then, during the first week of school, woke up sobbing in the middle of the night. When I asked her why she was crying, she said she dreamed that a dinosaur was chasing her. Both undergraduate and graduate students have comparable *monsters that chase them.*

When I asked students in my dramatic writing class to talk about their fears, the thousand faces of fear began to emerge. For these upper-level students, fear presented itself as fear of becoming "de-institutionalized"—fear of independence and fear of leaving the security of the university. These students mentioned some of the usual suspects as well: fear of being misunderstood and fear of change. Interestingly, these very talented students also identified a fear of success.

Several years earlier, when one of these students had been a high school senior and was deciding where to enroll, I had asked him where his academic and professional dream would take him. First, he asked if I was serious. When I assured him that I really wanted to know, he said he wanted to end up in the director's chair in Hollywood. I urged him to choose the university where he could establish not only a clear professional trajectory but could also establish a deep personal and social identity, so that if he achieved success in Hollywood, he would be able to handle it.

Some students are stopped far short of the fear of success, and even short of the fear of failure, by having to face the fear of parental disapproval. Several years ago, a student in my department came to me for academic advising. She said that her mother wanted her to major in public relations. I asked her what she wanted to do. She repeated that her mother wanted her to pursue public relations. After I made several more requests to learn her own preference, she quietly suggested that she would like to pursue acting, but quickly said again what her mother had chosen for her. I soon realized that either the student, or the mother, or both were in the grip of fear.

From the heart of the heart of learning, a pedagogy of love enables us to present a thousand images of divine love—images that transcend and transform fear. Rainer Maria Rilke, for example, reminds us that the love of God anchors us in relationship—that we are not alone:

> God speaks to each of us as he makes us,
> then walks with us silently out of the night. (1996, p. 88)

In the poem, Rilke affirms the full drama of human experience—its "beauty and terror"—and affirms that God accompanies us through all of it. In the vicissitudes of both failure and success, I can affirm that "I am a child of God. I am not alone." This simple and profound affirmation, this consciousness, enhances gratitude, patience, and humility, and provides resources for encountering suffering and mystery.

Teaching students to encounter ultimate questions and mysteries provides a qualitative dimension to whatever subject or course students have signed up for. Engaging students in the great mysteries of human experience and of the physical world will enlarge the context for any particular class or academic discipline. For example, recent studies of the Big Bang theory have forced scientists not only to ask how the Big Bang occurred but *why*, and, therefore, why we are here. The new success of cosmologists in exploring the depth and history of the universe makes unavoidable the questions of where we come from and where we are going—and the purpose of human existence. According to University of Chicago cosmologist Michael Turner, "'The No. 1 question, the question above all other questions, is why are we here'" (Kotulak, p. 1). This widely asked and unavoidable question is a profoundly spiritual question. This question provides a qualitative context for the courses and disciplines we teach.

In the words of the old gospel song, this "Love that will not let me go" enables the greatest and most profound learning available to us as human beings. Because God is love, rather than fear, I approach teaching in holistic ways. I try to address not only the academic requirements of particular courses, but students' immediate, complex learning situations, such as illness or a death in the family, as well as the host of ultimate questions to which their lives will respond across time.

From my mother and her extended family, I have also learned that life is a story. Learning to live out of love rather than fear requires us to negotiate and co-create our own stories—to accept what we must and change what we can. It allows us to reconcile ourselves with our own stories. In *Casing a Promised Land*, H. L. Goodall writes that "we cannot have an identity of our own until we have our own story" (1994, p. 170). Knowing and taking responsibility for my own story enables me to connect course and learning goals to students' lives, enabling students to examine and develop their central story and identity. Rumi (1995), the thirteenth-century poet and mystic, frequently focuses on the process of how we make our personal journeys—the whirling epiphanies and unexpected transformations which leap beyond our goals and intentions. In "Unfold Your Own Myth," he writes:

Who gets up early to discover the moment light begins?
Who finds us here circling, bewildered, like atoms?
Who comes to a spring thirsty
and sees the moon reflected in it?
Who, like Jacob blind with grief and age,
smells the shirt of his lost son
and can see again?
Who lets a bucket down and brings up
a flowing prophet? Or like Moses goes for fire
and finds what burns inside the sunrise?

Jesus slips into a house to escape enemies,
and opens a door to the other world.
Solomon cuts open a fish, and there's a gold ring.
Omar storms in to kill the prophet
and leaves with blessings. . . .

But don't be satisfied with stories, how things
have gone with others. Unfold your own myth, without complicated explanation,
so everyone will understand the passage,
We have opened you.

Start walking toward Shams. Your legs will get heavy
and tired. Then comes a moment
of feeling the wings you've grown,
lifting. (pp. 40–41)

As teachers, we provide the learning contexts in which students can unfold and create their own stories. I often tell students that I have high expectations for attendance—not because every class session will inspire them (or even justify their tuition bills), but because I have no way to know, in advance, which class sessions will create spiritual, intellectual, or emotional fire. Who can say where or when learning will strike?

As teachers, we can place students in situations in which profound learning becomes possible—situations in which they self-consciously co-create their own stories. Dietrich Bonhoeffer, the great German theologian and pacifist killed by the Nazis for his participation in a plot to assassinate Hitler, describes the situation in which "faith becomes possible" (1963). In Bonhoeffer's retelling of the biblical story, Jesus' disciples have been fishing all night on the Sea of Galilee, and they have caught nothing. Jesus appears to them, walking on the water. Peter decides he wants to imitate this miracle. He steps out of the boat and onto the water, and begins to sink. At that moment, Bonhoeffer declares, faith becomes possible for Peter.

As teachers, we enable the most profound learning for our students when we create the contexts and situations in which learning becomes possible—situations in which learning is existential and appropriately challenging. One year, on sabbatical, I served as a faculty sponsor for an eight-week trip to Morelia, Mexico. Because our second-grader had studied Spanish since kindergarten, my wife and I placed her in a bilingual school. After two days she declared, with eloquent gestures, that the Spanish was above her head, the English was at her knees, and, holding her hand at eye level, she said she needed instruction right there. Teaching from the heart enables us to hear students locate their learning level or circumstance and to take it into account.

Indeed, the drama of existential learning often carries elements of real or perceived danger. For several years I taught at a small, rural college that offered a January interterm. Each January, I took students to live in and rehab apartments in the 14th Street corridor of Washington, DC, an area still boarded up from the riots which followed the assassination of Martin Luther King in 1968. On one of these interterms, I discovered that some of the students had been so scared by their first exposure to urban poverty that they had spent the first evening moving all the furniture in the apartment to barricade the front door. The next day I had to convince several students not to leave the city. I had to close the too-wide gap between those students' previous experiences (their stories) and the story of poverty and its discontents in Washington, DC. The transformation of fear had to occur before genuine learning could become possible.

Storytelling, careful listening, and relational learning do have the potential for making significant changes in students' lives. Several years ago, in my seminar on ethnography and intercultural performance, the class interviewed several Palestinian refugees living near our campus in Chicago. After one of these interviews, a black South African student told me that participating in the interview had been very important, even liberating for him. I asked why. He said, "Listening to that person's story, I realized that my people are not the only ones who have suffered." Apparently he had placed his prior experiences in a larger context, opening new possibilities both for self-understanding and for empathy with the experience of others.

Indeed, learning to live out of love rather than fear enables us to move toward the stories and needs of others—learning truth-telling, empathy, compassion, justice, transformation, and reconciliation. As part of my own journey toward the conflicts and suffering of others, I developed an oral history project in the Middle East, recording the stories of older Palestinians who lost their land in 1948, when the state of Israel was created. I developed a play, *The Longing,* based on these stories, and produced it for three years with student performers. Recently, one of those students came to me and said, "When I came to this university, I didn't know anything about the Middle East. Now I want to complete a minor in Middle East Studies." Teaching and learning from love and truth-telling leads one toward transformation of the self and engagement in the real world. In *Pedagogy of the Oppressed,* Paulo Freire suggests that "the important thing is the continuing transformation of reality, in behalf of the continuing humanization of men [and women]" (2000, p. 81).

It is crucial to remember that not all of the "oppressed" are poor or marginalized. Some of our spiritually oppressed students have high SAT scores and attend our classes. In a class that I taught on "The Rhetoric of War and Peace," one student objected to my requirement that students work out and declare their own ethical basis for the use or nonuse of violence to create social change or to maintain the status quo. In his final course evaluation, the student wrote, "Quit making us make ethical choices." Every time I have taught this course or similar courses, I begin with this anecdote. I make clear that the course will involve a journey of moral and ethical decision making.

The heart of the heart of learning involves not only the capacity to make moral and ethical decisions; it involves the capacity to find and act upon the interplay of truth-telling, the pursuit of justice, forgiveness, mercy, and reconciliation. In the tradition of the Hebrew prophets, we are required "to do justice, seek mercy, and to walk humbly with God" (Micah 6:8). Daniel Hartnett, a Jesuit who worked with the poor of Peru for 25 years, writes that the pursuit of justice involves listening, narratives, relationships, analysis, and action. He writes that "In the area of justice, the turn (or return) to experience has a narrative quality. . . . It means real contact with those who suffer the effects of structural injustice" (2003, p. 1). He suggests that "the first step toward justice begins with listening to narratives of injustice." However, there is a qualitative shift when the careful listening also involves direct contact with the narrator of injustice. Such contact and listening is necessary, he suggests, in order for justice to be achieved, because "justice is an affect, a basic moral sentiment, a matter of the heart" (p. 2).

Learning to live out of love rather than fear takes us toward empathy, the ability to feel with and to walk alongside the experiences of others— their hopes, fears, cultural expressions, history, and suffering. Empathy is a central dynamic in my teaching of storytelling and other performance classes. However, as Hartnett reminds us, empathy and a feeling for the narratives of others takes on another dimension when students are enabled to meet the narrators, especially the narrators of injustice and oppression. Face-to-face narration and listening create relationships. Relationships with those who suffer create moral obligations. Moral obligations generate analysis of complex situations and active responses. The learning process moves from the head to the heart and toward compassionate analysis and action. The student may ask, "How has this person suffered? Why has this person been oppressed? What systems create or maintain this oppression? What can I do to change or transform this situation?"

If we, as teachers, have the courage to engage ourselves, our research, and our teaching in the suffering of the world, we will move into the heart of learning and engage our students in the drama of human experience. In this way, we can feed the imagination of the world with a vision of justice and conflict transformation. For many years I have taught students how to record and study the stories of people who have lived through major conflicts—in Bosnia, Israel, Palestine, South Africa, and elsewhere. Just before the Second Intifada, I took a group of students to Israel and Palestine for a course presumptuously called "Conflict Transformation in the Middle East." Among other student transformations that occurred, one of those students entered law school to study international law and human rights. Teaching from love and from the heart draws us progressively into the narratives of others, toward truth-telling, analysis of unjust systems, and efforts to create a more just world order.

Learning to reconcile oneself to God, to co-create one's own story, and to work for liberty and justice for all can only be sustained over the long haul through "communities of the spirit." These communities—intellectual, spiritual, and socially engaged—sustain us and enable us to learn with others and to act for others. Because of this, I frequently require students to work in teams on case studies or other large projects which they could not develop alone—projects such as an ethnography of the homeless, or the "lost boys of Sudan" who live near our Chicago campus, or the 30,000 Bosnian refugees who also live nearby. To be socially and politically engaged for the long haul, we must find and participate in "communities of the spirit." Rumi (1995) writes:

> There is a community of the spirit.
> Join it, and feel the delight
> of walking in the noisy street,
> and *being* the noise.
>
> Drink *all* your passion,
> and be a disgrace.
>
> Close both eyes
> to see with the other eye.
>
> Open your hands,
> if you want to be held.
>
> Sit down in this circle.
>
> Quit acting like a wolf, and feel
> the shepherd's love filling you. . . .
>
> Be empty of worrying.
> Think of who created thought!
>
> Why do you stay in prison
> when the door is so wide open?
>
> Move outside the tangle of fear-thinking.
> Live in silence.
>
> Flow down and down in always
> widening rings of being. (p. 3)

To live a full life, Rumi suggests, one must join the dance of community, the community of the spirit. Without deep connections to communities of the spirit, we will present signs of ill health and "fear-thinking" to the world—depression, anxiety, loneliness, underachievement, and overachievement.

Even for those of us who have grown up in communitarian traditions, we frequently forget the call of community and the limits of individualism in our lives. After 13 years of living in one place, my family recently began the arduous task of moving—fixing up the old house, sorting, packing, renovation of the new house, and moving—a huge and complex process, one that I knew the four of us could not accomplish by ourselves. Tentatively, I began to consider whether the men's group to which I have belonged for nine years might be a source of assistance. When I asked the leader of the group if it would be appropriate for me to ask the rest of the group for help, he responded, "Absolutely; you should insist on it." Even though this is a group with long-lasting commitments to each other, I had worried about whether my family's needs were great enough to make a claim on the busy lives of these men—a medical doctor, a father of twins, a chemist, and others. If we are constrained, even afraid, to ask our communities for what we need, we will suffer the loneliness and fears which run deep in American culture.

However, finding an adequate spiritual foundation, learning reconciliation with oneself, and thinking globally is much more than a personal task. Learning how to act on behalf of others over the long haul requires connections to communities of the spirit—communities of reflection, interpretation, and action. Communities of the spirit are communities of conscience that draw us beyond our personal preoccupations, beyond personal spiritual renewal, toward visions of the global village, the peaceable kingdom, and liberty and justice for all. To inform students about the suffering of the world without providing access to communities of the spirit is to create burdens which most individuals cannot bear.

We can develop such communities and invite students to become active participants. Several years ago, sitting in a restaurant overlooking the Sea of Galilee, a colleague of mine proposed that several of us create a conflict transformation program. For nearly two years, an interdisciplinary faculty group gathered to discuss the philosophy and practical dimensions of such a program. Over time, this voluntary working group—drawn from the humanities, social sciences, religious studies, and business—became a community of the spirit. As we worked together, we often discussed how students learn nonviolence and conflict transformation as a way of life, which is much more than a set of techniques. We concluded that students would be required to choose a particular community and complete an internship with that community, in order to observe and participate in conflict transformation as a way of life.

We must help build the bridges between individual journeys, the classroom, and communities of spirit and social action. In my experience, many students do not know the organizations or resources within their own religious traditions or local communities that provide a social service or work for justice or some form of conflict transformation. Calling students to connect with the best of their religious, ethnic, or other communities is vital for sustaining the journey toward reconciliation. As Claudia Horwitz (2002) suggests in *The Spiritual Activist,* one can also create new communities of the spirit, "circles," or small groups of individuals who "gather regularly, with intention, to support each other, renew themselves spiritually, and explore areas of common interest. . . . These groups matter because they provide a space in which people can heal from the past, learn to honor what is truly present, and envision a radically different future" (p. 176).

As we ourselves learn to "move outside the tangle of fear-thinking," we can lead our students to transform their fears, to entertain ultimate questions, such as "Why are we here?" to recognize that we are not alone, to cocreate their own stories, to actively respond to the world's narratives of suffering and oppression, and to sustain themselves through communities of reflection and action. The heart of the heart of learning is the journey from fear toward love—the love of God, the love of self, the love of others, and the love of communities of justice, mercy, and humble spirituality.

References

Bonhoeffer, D. (1963). *The cost of discipleship* (2nd ed.). (R. H. Fuller, Trans.). New York: Macmillan.

Freire, P. (2000). *Pedagogy of the oppressed.* New York: Continuum. (Original work published 1970)

Goodall, H. L. (1994). *Casing a promised land: The autobiography of an organizational detective as cultural ethnographer.* Carbondale: Southern Illinois University Press.

Hartnett, D. S. J. (2003). Arm-in-arm for justice. In E. D. Asch & S. K. Walsh (Eds.), *Defining justice, imagining justice, doing justice.* Shared text project 2003 (pp. 1–3). Chicago: Loyola University Chicago.

Horwitz, C. (2002). *The spiritual activist: Practices to transform your life, your work, and your world.* New York: Penguin Compass.

Kotulak, R. (2003, August 3). A cosmic puzzle. *Chicago Tribune,* sec. 2, p. 1.

Rilke, R. M. (1996). *Rilke's book of hours: Love poems to God* (A. Barrows & J. Macy, Trans.). New York: Riverhead Books.

Rumi, J. (1995). *The essential Rumi* (C. Barks, Trans.). San Francisco: HarperCollins.

Unceasing Change Turns the Wheel of Life

When I was a student in junior high, I decided that people in school were alienated, both the "good" students and the "poor" students, as well as the teachers. Moreover, I was learning little, even though I was motivated to learn, and even when I was appearing to achieve, I was mainly going through motions to meet someone else's approval. So I set out to be an influence of change, a goal that got me through college and my earliest teaching positions and into positions of leadership as a reading resource teacher, a district reading coordinator, and a school principal.

During this period of time I was also becoming increasingly influenced by Buddhist thought. I meditated sporadically and read a number of books by Buddhists. I also sought out friends who practiced Buddhism and enjoyed learning of their perspectives. I sometimes referred to myself as a BuU (pronounced "boo yoo"), to reflect the influence of Buddhism on my Unitarian Universalist beliefs. From these experiences I gained insights that have influenced my thinking about educational change. Three that are most significant are: Change is constant for everyone; it is best when I am not attached to my goals for educational change; and it is counterproductive to think of good and bad in teaching.

Constant Change

Despite a good deal of effort on my part to promote change in education, too often I felt that the change I desired was not occurring. I frequently felt resentful about this and sometimes felt that others resented me for my efforts. Thus, with my head full of questions, I went back to graduate school to seek answers. I began my doctoral program knowing that I wanted to study school change, particularly teacher change, and that did indeed become the focus of my dissertation work. Along the way I found myself reading voluminously on the topic, and I found myself frequently thinking of instances of non-change that I had experienced in my career.

At the same time, I was being influenced by the thinking of Buddhist teachers and practitioners. One day during my graduate studies I took a break from my "scholarly" reading and picked up one of the many Buddhist books I had acquired in the previous few years. In it, Buddhist teacher Elaine Boorstein (1995) reflected upon the constantly changing nature of reality, reminding me of Buddha's observation as he sat under the bodhi tree, that we are caught in the endless flow of time, just as a river is endlessly flowing. We are not standing still, we are always in flow, moving through life and constantly changing, however subtly.

I mentally nodded in agreement with Boorstein (1995) and then was struck by a contradiction: In one part of my life, my graduate studies, I struggled to understand why people don't change and in another part of my life, my spiritual pursuits, I accepted that life is a matter of continual flow, of constant change. How could I hold both ideas in my head at the same time and what did I want to do about this?

This moment was a turning point in my thinking about teacher change. I decided to try applying the Buddhist notion of continual flow to my view of teachers. I was feeling quite successful in this effort until I thought of Bob, a teacher I had worked with while I was an administrator. My view of Bob was that he was stuck. His lessons were so similar year to year that I had once joked with a colleague that I could set my calendar by noting which days Bob was beginning each of his social studies units. In addition, Bob appeared resistant to most schoolwide efforts at change. He even dressed the same every day.

I found it difficult to apply the notion of constant change to Bob until I recalled a conversation he and I had once had. He came to see me because he was concerned that a district-wide reorganization was on the horizon and that it might require him to move to a new school and grade level. His question for me was about how soon I thought that change might take place. "I wouldn't mind moving to a new school at this time," Bob explained, "but in a few years when I'm closer to retirement, it might be difficult. I won't be as adaptable to change at that time."

I endeavored to prevent my jaw from dropping as I realized that Bob perceived himself as someone who presently made changes with ease. He didn't see himself as stuck—he saw change as a part of his everyday experience! I couldn't make sense of this, and didn't try, until years later when I reflected upon Boorstein's conceptions of our constantly changing nature.

After considerable thought I have come to believe that everyone is indeed changing, even those who appear stuck, like Bob. An interesting aspect of Bob's life is that he had just seen his only child off to college and also had just dealt with the death of his mother-in-law, who had lived with Bob and his wife. Talk about a lot of change in a short period of time! When one looks at a person as a whole being rather than looking at just one aspect of that person's life, such as his or her role as a teacher, one can more easily see the change that is a constant for all of us.

This re-conceptualization of change has significantly influenced my approach to teachers with whom I am working. I no longer divide the population of teachers (or any other population) into those who change and those who are stuck. I approach teachers with the belief that they all change, that they are all in the process of change. Some move more quickly, or do it more visibly, or change at work instead of other parts of their lives, but all change. This realization has prevented me from giving up on some teachers. It also enables me to see smaller, quieter changes more easily.

Not long after I read Boorstein, while doing my graduate studies, I was in a course on educational change. During the first class period, groups of students were asked to depict their understandings of change on large pieces of paper. I persuaded my group to write this maxim, a variation of Descartes' famous dictum that, "I think, therefore I am." My group wrote, "I change, therefore I am."

Nonattachment to Bringing Change About

I was an elementary school principal for eight years. During that time I tried to bring about change in two schools. I worked very hard and was usually frustrated, sometimes angry, often defeated. More recently I have worked as a consultant with the staff of an elementary school 60 miles from my university. I have been much more successful in bringing change to that elementary school. This success is due to several factors, but one important contributor is that I don't care too much about what happens at that school. I am not indifferent—I wish the best for the staff and students of that school—but I do not *care,* in the sense that I am not worried about undesirable outcomes or the absence of the outcomes I wish for.

The Buddhist notion of nonattachment informs this stance, particularly nonattachment to an expected outcome. Shunryu Suzuki (1970) advises that one empty one's mind of expected outcomes. He states:

> As long as we have some definite ideas about or some hope in the future, we cannot really be serious with the moment that exists right now. . . . Even though you are not trying so hard, you expect that some promising thing will come, as long as you follow a certain way. But there is no certain way that exists permanently. There is no way set up for us. Moment after moment we have to find our own way. Some idea of perfection, or some perfect way which is set up by someone else, is not the true way for us. (p. 111)

Suzuki's statement leads me to recognize that, in my work with teachers, I understand best when I have no expectations of what is to occur. An attitude of nonattachment to a particular idea, practice, or curricular innovation enables me to be present with teachers and others as they seek to understand the work they are doing and explore changes that may occur. When I am focused on the outcome that I desire, I am unable to see what is going on around me and unable to respond in the moment to those with whom I am working. My attention is occupied by my goal. In fact, my purpose in being present is entirely altered when I detach from my desired outcome. I shift from being present only to move ahead to being present for the purpose of being present.

An additional problem with desire for a pre-ordained outcome is that it leads to fear. After all, there is no guarantee that that outcome will be reached, and if it is not, negative experiences might result. For instance, I could seem incompetent, or the teachers with whom I am working could become frustrated, or those who are paying me could feel disappointed. When I work in fear I am not engaged with those around me; I am engaged with fear. Fear serves as a lens through which everyone and everything appear to be a threat, and I respond in a defensive posture. This produces anger, anxiety, tension, and mistrust. It does not facilitate growth among educators.

Finally, in caring too much I leave myself vulnerable to dissatisfaction with circumstances. If I want the school, classroom, or curriculum to be so much different, I become critical of what is and frustrated by anything short of the outcomes I seek. I am assisted in the struggle to avoid this dissatisfaction by a story told by Mark Epstein. Epstein, a psychotherapist and Buddhist, tells of a retreat interview with Joseph Goldstein, a meditation teacher, who responds to Epstein's dissatisfaction with the way the retreat is going by telling him:

> You know what I sometimes do?. . . I pretend that I'm dying and that there's nothing to be done. Rather than judging it, take no position in your mind. Stop leaning into circumstances . . . and rest in your own awareness. (Epstein, 1998, p. 116)

This story reminds me that an attitude of non-judgment will prevent me from feeling frustrated at a lack of desired outcomes. A stance of non-attachment will enable me to be aware of what is happening and respond to that rather than responding to my fear and dissatisfaction about an unmet goal.

Neither Good Nor Bad, Just Teachers

A great obstacle to working successfully with teachers has been eliminating the notion that some teachers are good and some are not. This idea seems nearly inherent in the concept of promoting changed teaching practices—after all, why would one want to see change if one did not see some current practices as ineffective, harmful, or bad? However, separating the world of teaching into those who are good teachers and those who are bad teachers leads to dangerous attitudes and counterproductive interactions.

A distinction might be made between good and bad practices and good and bad teachers. It is a fairly familiar distinction to make: Love the person, hate the behavior. However, from a Buddhist perspective one would not divide the world into good and bad whether speaking of people or behaviors. Buddhist thinking avoids dualism and seeks instead to understand the interconnectedness of all.

It seems to be in our human nature to have the desire to separate the world into good and bad. In addition, though, I suspect that there is something about the teaching profession that encourages such judgment. Part of the discourse of teaching all too often involves a determination of "good" students, "best" practices, "high" test scores, and so forth. We are encouraged as educators to be judgmental.

In the field of educational change, this inclination to judge has led to the labeling of some individuals as resisters, as those not worthy of our attention, or at least not ready for it. There is a maxim that one should not "waste one's time" with resisters. Inherent in such ideas is also the notion that some individuals, because their beliefs or practices are not what we wish them to be, are inferior, lazy, or difficult.

I find these ideas to be morally repugnant as well as ineffective. I'm reminded of the ethical considerations in such judgments when I read the work of the Dalai Lama. For instance, the Dalai Lama has written of the high value of altruism in Buddhist practice. One should, he says, aim for "compassion towards all sentient beings equally. Compassion here means the wish that all other beings should be free of suffering" (2000, p. 58).

From an ethical point of view, it makes sense to me that I should not dismiss some people as inferior. However, I also know that such judgment of good and bad teachers and teaching is ineffective as well. It alienates others. No matter how subtle, if I am thinking in such a dualistic and judgmental manner, I convey it in my manner. In addition, when I dismiss some teachers, I fail to take the time to understand what they are doing and why they do it.

Again, the Dalai Lama helps me with this idea. He writes of the importance of understanding cause and effect:

> The reason that the Buddhist teachings emphasize the importance of cause and effect is not because it is some kind of divine law, but rather because it provides a deeper understanding of the nature of reality. Why do Buddhists come to this conclusion? Because we know from our experience, and through observation, that things and events do not arise randomly. They respect a certain order. (2000, p. 18)

We all do seem to understand the notion of cause and effect, except that in everyday life we seem to attribute the cause of behavior we don't agree with as a reflection of a flaw in the individual displaying that behavior. For example, a teacher who has not adopted a particular practice may be labeled

as lazy or uncaring about the success of the students. The Buddhist emphasis on both compassion and cause and effect causes me to try to see positive reasons for all teachers' behaviors.

For example, I once worked in a school that became divided about how
to best teach children to read. The leader of the perspective opposite of
mine was a woman named Beth. The colleagues on "my side" and I
thought Beth was a terrible teacher; we criticized and even made fun of
her. I left that school, as did one of my closest colleagues, but this colleague and I met occasionally for lunch. Inevitably, our conversation
would lead to the turmoil we experienced in that school and our continuing insights about what had happened. One year as we discussed these past
events, my colleague and I came to the same realization: Beth believed
every bit as much in the correctness of her view as we did in ours. She believed that her practices were best for children, just as we believed ours
were best. In retrospect, I am rather embarrassed that it took me so long to
arrive at this realization, and I am sure my judging got in the way.

I now understand that neither Beth nor I was the "good" teacher. There
was a cause for each of us to believe something different about reading instruction, and to each of us our beliefs were "right." This insight has
helped me to listen more carefully to teachers whose views I do not share.
I often find that these teachers are motivated by their care for children,
something virtually all teachers share. Of course there are other reasons
why teachers choose the practices they do, but if I listen carefully, I can
understand how these choices make sense to that person in that situation.

When I withhold judgment, listen, and seek an understanding of the
cause of teachers' beliefs and practices, I am able to respond more genuinely to the person with whom I am working, rather than responding to a
"bad" or "lazy" teacher. The latter response often leads me to be short,
angry, or defensive. The former response makes me more able to engage
with the person and to have a meaningful conversation about our beliefs
and practices. Frequently, too, I find that we have more in common than I
had thought. For instance, I once assisted teachers in an elementary school
in considering whether they wanted to change their practices for teaching
spelling. I found myself agreeing with those who wanted to teach spelling
in the context of children's writing, but I listened carefully to a woman
who wanted to preserve the use of a spelling workbook. This woman explained through tears that her son was not a good speller and that she did
not want other children to have to struggle so hard. I realized that we were

both motivated by a desire to help children struggle less. From this shared interest, we were able to explain more calmly—and listen more carefully—to the reasons why each of us saw a particular method as having more potential to reduce student failure. The nature of the conversation shifted from "I'm right, you're wrong," to, "We share a goal, now how can we get there?"

A Beginning

The insights I have shared are a beginning, in two ways. First, I have not mastered any of the efforts I describe. I continue to slip into practices in which I think of a teacher as stuck or "bad" or become attached to a desired outcome. This is indeed practice, in the sense that I must continue to engage with such efforts over and over again. Eventually, I will become more adept, but my focus must be on the present and on engaging in this practice.

I am cautious in this practice, because I don't want to feel superior nor do I want to use Buddhist thinking to mask "true" feelings underneath the language of compassion and non-attachment. Again, I must practice, in order to live the ideas I find appealing and useful.

In addition, these insights are a beginning because surely there are many additional ways in which Buddhist thinking can influence my work. The popularity of Buddhism in the West has made numerous texts and teachers available to the average person. The wisdom offered by these resources will continue to enrich my work and my practice.

The words of Charlotte Joko Beck help me to put these ideas in perspective:

> In the service we do, one of the dedications states, "Unceasing change turns the wheel of life." Experiencing, experiencing, experiencing; change, change, change. "Unceasing change turns the wheel of life, and so reality is shown in all its many forms. Peaceful dwelling as change itself liberates all suffering sentient beings and brings them to great joy." (pp. 119–120)

The entire concept of educational change could be challenged by Buddhist beliefs. It could seem contradictory to seek the focus on the moment which is so often encouraged by Buddhist practices and yet to attend to the future of education. Conversely, the reality of constant change, which is reflected in schools as well as everywhere else, means that change is occurring. In fact, as Joko Beck reminds us, this change "turns the wheel of life"—it is inherent to existence. And what is the Buddhist response? Peaceful dwelling in change. As an educator, I seek not to be a "change agent" nor to resist change—in other words, I don't want to pretend that I have a choice to accept change, cause change, or stop change. Rather, I want to recognize that joy will come from peaceful dwelling in change.

References

Beck, C. J. (1993). *Nothing special: Living Zen.* San Francisco: Harper.

Boorstein, S. (1995). *It's easier than you think: The Buddhist way to happiness.* San Francisco: Harper.

Epstein, M. (1998). *Going to pieces without falling apart: A Buddhist perspective on wholeness.* New York: Broadway.

His Holiness the XIV Dalai Lama. (2000). *Transforming the mind: Teachings on generating compassion.* London: Thorsons.

Suzuki, S. (1970). *Zen mind, beginner's mind: Informal talks on Zen meditation and practice.* New York: Weatherhill.

PART II

TRANSFORMING PRACTICES

Tale of a Sorcerer's Apprentice

The Lesson

I reached across the table to ladle some fish soup over my breakfast of warm rice and spied Master Suh standing in the doorway of the small kitchen. The sun was shining in the little window that looked out onto Ellis Street from the second story of the converted parking garage. I had been living in Master Suh's martial art gym in downtown San Francisco for nearly two months. I had recently earned my first-degree black belt. I had been Master Suh's student for almost six years. I was 29 years old.

On this day Master Suh was in one of his rare effusive moods. At times like these his *chi* radiated like a warm sunny day. Smiling, he called me over for a chat. As I approached the old master, with my newly acquired black belt tied firmly and confidently around my waist, I was wary. Ever since I had received my black belt in a ceremony a week earlier my status in the gym had changed dramatically. My Korean instructors treated me differently. They were more serious now. They shouted orders at me and gave me a list of new responsibilities—most of which entailed cleaning of one kind or another. This was the real life version of "wax on . . . wax off." No one had warned me that it was coming and no one offered a clue as to what it all meant. But that's how it was in Master Suh's gym. Our Korean teachers rarely engaged in verbal explanations. You were told what to do and you did it. If you had questions you were rebuffed. Questions, I had learned, were interpreted as a lack of loyalty and respect. One of the outcomes of this approach was that you were kept constantly on your toes. The "no questions" rule meant that you were operating in a highly ambiguous context most of the time. Add to that the intercultural dimension of the everyday communication, and you can begin to see how challenging the learning environment truly was.

So when Master Suh called me over for a chat, I was expecting anything. My first thought was that he had some nasty job for me—which he often did—like painting his friend's store or helping a family move into a new apartment. Instead the old man stepped forward and put his arm around my shoulder. He pulled me in close like I was his little grandchild. He was teasing me and started to laugh as he watched me squirm uncomfortably in a grip that was like iron. This was another thing that made you wary of Master Suh; he was incredibly strong and unthinkably quick. If he wanted to show you how effective some technique was there was no way you could avoid the contact or slip past what was headed your way. Maybe that was one of his teaching secrets; to keep you always on your guard expecting the unexpected. More likely it was just his way of amusing himself at your expense.

So there I squirmed, tense, expectant, and locked in his grip. He eased his hold a bit, smiled one of his most boyish grins and said:

William . . . you are a black belt now. You need to teach. Starting on Monday you will teach the children's class . . . every day.

Once again I was taken by surprise. I had not expected to be teaching any classes, especially the dreaded children's class. For the past few months I had watched my Korean instructors try to handle the thirty or so kids that showed up each afternoon for their lessons. I wanted no part of it. The kids had near-zero attention spans with off-the-chart energy. I knew intuitively and empirically that this was a deadly combination that would cause me no end of pain. The worst part was that there was no way to say "no" to Master Suh. It just wasn't done. If he told you to do something you just did it. This was another of Master Suh's traits that bedeviled his senior students. The more senior you were the harder it was to say "no."

Sensing my dread over the thought of teaching the children's class, Master Suh smiled again, this time with more concern and less mischief. He seemed to know what I was feeling, which was often the case with him. Those who had been around long enough knew that the old man was totally psychic. The art of reading others' thoughts and feelings was just one of many esoteric techniques that the advanced Korean instructors engaged in as part of their training.

> William . . . a black belt has to learn to teach. Don't worry . . . you will be a good teacher. But teaching is not easy. Fighting is easy! In six months I can make you a champion fighter. But to be a good teacher takes years . . . teaching is very complicated. Even so . . . there is only one thing you need to know:
>
> "love flows". . .

He patted me on the shoulder and told me to finish my breakfast—that was my first lesson on teaching.

Interpretation

Today, I am an assistant professor in a college of education that is known for its strong teacher preparation program. I teach graduate and undergraduate courses in philosophy, ethics, and policy analysis. In the twenty years that have elapsed since Master Suh explained teaching to me in terms of "love" and "flow" I don't think I've once walked into a classroom without saying the words silently to myself. I do this unconsciously, yet with the understanding that by placing this intention in my mind and in my body, my spirit is given a path to follow.

When I first heard the words "love flows," I knew I did not understand them. At the time I just listed them among the many enigmas I had witnessed in Master Suh's gym. Over time, however, the words took root and I found myself often wondering about their meaning. Much as I tried, I simply could not grasp the lesson that I knew was there. The whole concept eluded me. However, the meaning seemed just beyond my horizon of comprehension.

It was not until five years later when I began teaching martial art in my own school that the words began to take on concrete sense. I was renting gym space by the hour and holding classes two nights a week in an old hall that was owned by a German-American civic club. To attract students I gave public demonstrations of my art in any venue that was available. With no advertising budget, no permanent facility, and no students, I learned how one could "grow" a teaching/learning environment from nothing but one's intention. After three years of hard work my martial art school had grown into a self-sustaining learning environment. Indeed, the truth of Master Suh's enigma began to unfold in front of me. I understood that love is something you share with others, that it is a foundation for relationships characterized by possibility. To say that "love flows" is to say that there is a stream of possibility. It is to say that there is action in intention. Understanding the meaning of the words became as simple as observing what happened when they were true. I may not be able to define what it means to say "love flows," but I certainly can feel when it happens.

Today I struggle to make love flow in my college classroom. However, I wonder whether I can make love flow in such a way that it will open up the possibility for future teachers to make love flow in their classrooms. My point of reflection always originates in Master Suh's gym. I did not know it at the time, but all of what I learned there was "slow learning." The kind of learning that takes years to cultivate before it flowers into something recognizable. A pedagogy like Master Suh's, which is based on the concept "love flows," is not something that can be grasped in an instant. One has to constantly reflect on two things: what is "love" and what is "flow," and then you have to push further to understand how one does "love flows."

How one does "love flows" is not easy to describe. In fact, I don't think there is a precise formula or approach that is right for everyone. However, I do think there are insights that I can share which may be useful for those who find that they too are beginning to walk down a journey of the heart in their teaching. For me, it is a question of how to align my teaching practice with my spiritual practice. As someone who did his graduate study in philosophy and communication, one thing I've learned is that metaphors, images, and symbols are essential to the work of aligning any aspect of life with matters of the spirit. In order to perceive and understand one's teaching as part of a spiritual whole it is crucially important, I think, to find the language and forms of communication that allow you to build that bridge. Language and patterns of communication are instrumental in shaping and constructing experience. Choosing to integrate everyday experience into a more meaningful whole is what spirituality is all about. A critical step in enacting this transformation involves using language and communication to breathe life into the ideal.

I actively seek out metaphors whose imagery can help me connect my everyday experience with my spiritual goals. Master Suh gave me the metaphor of "flow" to help me understand love in terms of what it can do and what it feels like. Two other images that can act as a bridge are the metaphors of the "heart" and of the "breath." Both of these images are prevalent in a number of spiritual and religious traditions. What these metaphors suggest is that our highest self is not a transcendental ideal but rather an experiential reality, one that can be enacted in the mundane world of the everyday. This is evident in the zen phrase "chop wood . . . carry water." It points to the idea that our spiritual practice can be enacted in the simple tasks that constitute everyday living. We don't have to carve out a separate place in our lives for spirituality. Likewise the image of a single heart beat—like that of the in-out cycle of a single breath—is a metaphor that tells us that being is becoming; the what of sacred being is grounded in the how of mundane becoming. The question of how "love flows" has become, for me, the question of how I bring my teaching in line with my heart. "Flow" is understood as from one heart to another.

Sometimes I think the question of how to do "love flows" can best be answered in the negative. How do we NOT do love flows? I think love does not flow when we attempt to reduce learning to quantifiable outcomes. It is not realized by reducing the work of students and teachers to a numeric value. I'm not arguing here against grades, though I would very much like to try teaching in a grade-free environment. What I am saying is this: policies that reduce teaching and learning to interchangeable units or outcomes that can be measured because they can be controlled is the opposite of "love flows." I will leave the debate concerning the proper place of evaluation and assessment to another essay. However, it seems clear to me that my spiritual goals are not furthered by a standards-based curriculum that obliterates any space for creativity and spontaneity in the classroom. While these instruments of reason and rationality may serve the needs of institutions, I have little doubt about their negative relation to the life of the spirit. In order to counteract the negative conditions cited above, I offer four positive approaches that I think will help you take the first steps toward teaching from the heart.

See What You Do as Spiritual Work

Think and talk about your teaching as a spiritual practice. Language and communication are everything! The language—the metaphors and images—you use to conceptualize and express your teaching to yourself and to others matters tremendously. Changing your teaching language and communication is a necessary step to teaching from the heart. This can be as simple as talking to colleagues about the "heart" of teaching or reflecting openly with others about what the "heart" of teaching really is. It also means self-reflection on the spiritual dimensions of teaching and learning. Start a journal in which you actively describe and interpret your teaching experience in spiritual terms. Ask yourself how your heart is touched by your everyday experiences in the classroom. Ask yourself what effect the organizational climate in your school is having on your spirit. Reflect on new policy initiatives in terms of what their spiritual impact will be on students, teachers, administrators, and other stakeholders.

Practice . . . Practice . . . Practice

Integrating your spiritual life with your work as a teacher is a holistic undertaking. You'll need to coordinate mind, body, and spirit. Walking the walk means moving your mind and your body in such a way that they too match the movement of your spirit. You can begin simply by asking yourself, "How do I teach from the heart?" In my view the answer lies in learning to trust your instincts and feel what is right. That means being spontaneous and intuitive. It's much like falling in love. You cannot get there instrumentally or incrementally. You have to allow it to happen. You have to let yourself fall. Now, I think it's fair to say that much of the institutional language and patterns of communication that shape how we operate as teachers makes this difficult. I know that in higher education the mind is privileged far beyond either the heart or the body. So to be an integrated or holistic teacher you have to step outside the dominant "language game" (as Wittgenstein would call it) and begin building an alternative discourse. It will help if you can find others to join you on the path. Experience has taught me that practicing one's art alone impedes your progress. It can be done, but the work is much harder and far less joyful. The same is true in teaching from the heart.

Structure Sets You Free

Ask yourself, "How do I establish my teaching as a spiritual practice?" Being a student of martial art I know that having "forms" or "structures" within which to practice greatly increases your ability to focus, concentrate, and be truly engaged on all levels. Martial art practice is often structured according to the familiar dance-like sequences that are so beautiful to watch when done well. We have all seen these highly choreographed maneuvers and know that there are many styles and traditions, each possessing their own unique characteristics. However, they all share some common elements. One of the most common features of forms practice is *repetition*. We can observe the effects or outcomes of repetition when the forms are done well. We easily notice the power and grace that comes from repeated practice. In martial art the forms are the essence of practice. They are choreographed and highly stylized in order to provide a structure that allows practitioners the freedom needed to release themselves from the constraints that are present when structure is absent.

The idea of a highly structured practice seems to contradict the idea of spontaneity that I emphasized above. There is a paradox at work here. The stylized predetermined sequences are highly structured, and yet they afford the practitioner an important degree of freedom. When forms are embodied repeatedly over time, the degree of freedom one experiences increases. The form, then, becomes a metaphor or model of the practice itself. It distills the essence of the whole through repetition of a simplified and easily controlled part. Through repetition of the part one is invited to take on the whole with greater focus and concentration. After months and years of practice the forms begin to grow from a small controllable space of embodiment into one of infinite range and variety.

In working to align our spiritual life with our work as teachers we need to establish patterns of activity that support and even mirror what it is we want to accomplish. If the plan is to integrate mind, body, and spirit, then we need to establish activities in our teaching that engage us and our students on all three levels. A first step might mean simply getting students away from their desks and moving. Martial art teaches that the mind and spirit can be engaged more readily through the indirect vehicle of the performing body. One way I do this in my classroom is to have students create and enact dramatic performances. I do this as early in the term as possible in order to set the tone for the weeks to come and also to instill the idea that our imaginations are going to be a vital resource during our course of study. For example, in my philosophy of education course we begin each semester by reading Paulo Freire's (1970/2000) classic indictment of teacher-centered education, *Pedagogy of the Oppressed*. Even though the text operates on a highly abstract conceptual level, I ask students to create a dramatic performance as a way to outline and summarize Freire's ideas. How is this teaching from the heart? First of all it gets the students' bodies and their imaginations involved in the process of learning. It also suggests to the students that I have faith in their creative abilities. More importantly, it indirectly asks the students to trust me because I am asking them to do something that many of them have never done before. I am asking them to make useful and productive links between reason and the imagination and to do so using a "playful" medium such as dramatic performance. I find that this exercise sets a precedent for learning through "heart-felt embodiment" and that it plays out in positive ways through the entire semester.

Another way that I teach from the heart is by talking about holistic and spiritual dimensions of teaching. I tell students that this is something I am engaged in as a teacher/scholar, and I ask them to describe their own experiences in classrooms that reflect these dimensions. I was surprised to find that many students have vivid recollections and stories about how they themselves have experienced teaching and learning from the heart. It is interesting to note that for many students these recollections go all the way back to their elementary school experience. Also of note is the clarity and ease with which students recall these experiences. It says something about the lasting impact that teaching from the heart can have on students.

A final thought on how we embody our teaching has to do with what our bodies say when we teach. If we are going to walk the walk, then we have to consider body language. There is no question that nonverbal communication speaks louder and more directly than words. Ask yourself this: "When I walk into my classroom each morning, what does my body say to students?" Does it say I trust you? Does it say I have confidence in your ability? Does it say that I have love in my heart? These are tough questions because they ask us to become conscious of our bodies in ways that our culture does not readily support. We rarely think of our bodies as tools of communication, and yet the research shows that our bodies do most of the talking. Teaching from the heart means using our bodies to express what is in our hearts. To do this we have to take stock of what we are doing with our bodies when we are teaching. For example, consider how you listen to students' responses during a discussion. What does your body reveal? Do you lean in or lean back when students respond? Are your arms folded across your chest? Is your posture inviting a response or resisting it? I am not advocating that we become method actors in our classrooms. However, the truth is that teaching, like everything else, is a performance. So why not take advantage of this fact, raise your level of awareness, and consider the ways your body can be used to communicate the spiritual dimensions of your teaching. While there are a number of excellent resources on nonverbal communication, including studies in the field of neuro-linguistic programming, perhaps the simplest way to begin is by reminding yourself each day what it is you wish to invoke through your teaching. With the help of old Master Suh I learned to organize my teaching practice around the principle of "love flows." Keeping this uppermost in my mind, I consciously and actively embody this intention in order to let it flow through me as it shapes my communication and classroom interaction.

Take Stock

It is natural to wonder if what we are doing is working or not. Because I take an experimental approach to teaching I'm constantly trying out new approaches. As a result I need to make careful observations and engage in constant reflection in order to do the work of improving the practice. I think of this as "polishing my mirror." In martial art this is often done during seated meditation. Sitting quietly and allowing one's thoughts to pass before the window of awareness is fundamental to developing one's practice. Ask yourself what you feel in your heart about your teaching. If you do this kind of reflection honestly and often, you will begin to construct a productive self-dialogue that will provide answers even as it raises new and even deeper questions. Keeping a journal record of this emerging dialogue will allow you to track changes and patterns of growth in your teaching.

The journey down the path of transformation will also be marked by changes that you can observe in others. I see concrete examples of my own transformation in the behaviors and attitudes displayed by my students. Recently, I have noticed a shift in how my students address one another during class discussions. Students make a great effort to learn and use each other's first names. Now this is not something that I had asked for or even encouraged. It simply grew out of a climate of mutual respect and regard that established itself within the classroom. What I find encouraging is that the discussions now feel much more personal and intimate. I interpret this as an indication that I am doing "love flows" slightly better than before.

Perhaps the clearest evidence that one is indeed teaching from the heart comes in the form of witness. It could be as simple as running into a student in the hall and hearing the words: "Hey Dr. Ashton, I want to thank you for your class . . . I know what I want to do with teaching now—I'm going to . . ." Maybe it is not the words so much as the smile behind them that says "love flows." Lately I've been hearing more directly from students in the form of emails and letters. Here's one from the days following September 11, 2001:

> Dr. Ashton,
> I just wanted to let you know how well I think you handled the recent tragedies in class. I have not been able to really "understand" the current state of our world, or talk about it in any other classes. You are one of the only teachers who has taken the time to let us all get everything on the table, let our frustrations, fears and feelings spill out. I somehow feel a sense of closure to this eternally opened issue/tragedy/surreal reality. I just wanted to say thanks.
>
> Kari

To hear directly from students about how they are affected by what goes on in your classroom can be a rare occurrence. A great deal of how we structure our communication with students seems to preclude these kinds of heartfelt messages. Nevertheless, the fact that they sometimes do appear is testimony to the fact that the spirit is alive and well in your practice.

Conclusions

The longer I teach the more I look at teaching selfishly. Today I insist that my own learning as well as that of the students occupy the center of what we do together. Practicing martial art has shown me that learning and teaching take place in a complex weave that is at a minimum comprised of communication, tradition, individual agency, and karma. I see my job as one of engaging purposefully and responsibly, with dedication and discipline, in a practice that co-generates and co-sustains an intentional communicative environment, one that allows each of us to identify his or her purpose and to work together toward its fulfillment. Even though teaching in a large public university places severe limits on the shape that my practice can take, my primary reason for teaching remains firmly grounded in the simple idea that each of us has a purpose in life that requires the help of others to fulfill. I believe, along with Paulo Freire and Martin Buber, that there is no "I" without a "Thou," and that the Self, which we experience as our own greatest possibility, is actually brought into existence exclusively through our interaction with the Other. This perspective allows me to see my teaching as a spiritual practice and to recognize the overwhelming importance of communication in fulfilling its purpose.

Building my teaching into a spiritual practice has become an essential dimension of integrating my personal and professional life. It has allowed me to discover deeper and more lasting satisfaction with the work I do and has enabled me to see my relationships with others as part of a larger more meaningful whole. In writing down these reflections I have tried to give you, the reader, some advice on how to build your own teaching into a spiritual practice. I suggested that one has to "talk the talk" and "walk the walk" in order to do "love flows." I tried to emphasize the importance of language and communication in shaping not only our discourse, but the very essence of who we are in the world. Borrowing a lesson from the martial arts I also noted that there is a productive contradiction in the paradoxical relation between structure and freedom in building one's practice. Finally, I acknowledged the need to assess one's efforts to teach from the heart. In all of this my primary goal has been to share some insights and to pass along some wisdom. It is my sincere hope that some of what I have said here about my own practice will be of value to the reader. If the path has been illuminated in any way by these words, then it is confirmation once again that indeed . . ."love flows."

Reference

Freire, P. (2000). *Pedagogy of the oppressed.* New York: Continuum. (Original work published 1970.)

CHAPTER 6

Inner Calm, Holistic Human Beings, and Life Purpose

As a second-year assistant professor of sociology, I find that I need all the skills at my disposal to assist me in keeping up with my work. My spiritual skills are among the important ones I draw on. They help me to stay in balance, to interact meaningfully with students, and to keep a useful perspective about what I'm doing. In this chapter, I will discuss three ways in which I feel my spirituality enhances my teaching.

First, I almost always meditate for ten minutes each morning. I became a big fan of meditation during graduate school, and used to set aside thirty minutes for it each day. When I began working full-time as a professor, I initially felt that I didn't have time in my life to meditate. I wasn't taking very good care of myself, working so much that I regularly cut into my sleep to prepare for classes and keep up with grading. After about seven months of frenzied activity, I attended a weekend conference on "joy," which reminded me of the importance of being in balance. I met a man at the conference who suggested that I set aside ten minutes each morning to meditate. I thought that I could spare ten minutes and promptly started doing it as part of my morning preparation for work.

There are lots of ways that people approach meditation, and it has been meaningful for me to experiment with several of them. Some meditations utilize candles and music, others involve recorded guided meditations, and still others use silence. Some people get a lot of benefit from meditating while walking, or working in their gardens. I have learned to meditate through participation in spiritual discussion groups, retreats, meditation classes, yoga, and martial arts. There are many books out about meditation, but I have learned primarily from other people with whom I have come in contact. Deepak Chopra's (1995) audiobook called *The Seven Spiritual Laws of Success* has also been very orienting for me. In my short morning meditations, the most important element for me is allowing my mind to quiet down, to be empty. I also usually move my attention upward, starting at my feet and ending above my head. I have heard this called the "elevator meditation," and it is a way of moving energy and attention to a higher level. As I end my meditations, I often choose the states of being (like peace, love, and joy) that I want to bring to my day.

It has been a year since I have started meditating again, and I have noticed many benefits that relate to teaching. I feel a much greater sense of inner calm. This calm helps me to listen better to the students because I have an outlet for the noise of my own thoughts. It also helps to reduce almost completely any defensiveness or fear that I may have when students ask questions or make comments in class. There are those occasional students who challenge material presented in the classroom. I now see in them an opportunity to further deepen a class conversation, and do not take their challenging remarks personally. This calm seems related to the sense of well-being that I get from my morning meditations. I am more confident now that student input can be used in a productive and educational manner. My attitude about this approach, facilitated by meditation, helps me to bring about a safe and respectful atmosphere in class, and an attentive ear when students visit me in my office. In general, I feel more capable of doing all the things I am trying to do. I feel a sense of confidence and peace about myself.

I remember one day last year when it dawned on me that the students were far more afraid of me than I was of them. Until then, I had been focused on my own tentative feelings about how my early attempts at teaching would be received. I came to realize that by being caught up in my own perspective, I had missed the big picture. This realization came about in a heavily experimental semester after I had asked students for some anonymous feedback about the course. The feedback from students led me to make some major changes to the course in the middle of that semester. I think many of the students were genuinely shocked that I had "heard" them and made changes accordingly. I believe that my meditative practice helped me to be in a more receptive space, allowing me to focus on where the students were coming from.

When I occasionally skip my morning meditation, I notice almost immediately that I feel a higher level of stress and anxiety. It is subtle, but I am easily aware of it. This helps me to realize the real benefits I receive from meditating, and to continue my commitment to this practice.

Meditation seems to bring me more clarity as well. I realize that my role as a teacher is not to fulfill my own attention needs, but to give attention to the students as much as possible, to give them a voice with which they can discover themselves. Some teachers seem to get caught up in the ego trip of hearing themselves talk (a lot), and I can now ask myself: For whom is it? I see a certain amount of my job being to create a space for reflection and discussion, and then get out of the way of students who find they have a lot to say. Students themselves can make some of my "brilliant" points in class if I can give them a space in which to say them.

Meditation is part of my larger effort to stay in balance in multiple areas of my life—spiritual, physical, intellectual, social, emotional, financial, and so forth. I consider my work as a professor to be like continuously training for a marathon. The idea is to learn to maintain my energy and momentum over the long haul. The semester is not a sprint! In a subtle way, I try to set an example for my students of how to be well rounded. Staying balanced helps me to maintain a helpful attitude toward the students as the semester wears on.

The second way I feel my spirituality enhances my teaching is in my recognition of students as holistic human beings, both inside and outside the classroom. I look for ways to support students in their lives, not just with the course topic. Inside the classroom, I do this by creating certain assignments in which students relate course material to their own lives. I also encourage discussions in which students can compare their attitudes and values to those of their peers. It helps that the courses I have taught (on marriage & family, and death & dying) can easily be related to students' own experiences. I see myself as a facilitator and discussion leader in addition to being one who presents information to students. Finding diverse ways to tap into the students' rich and varied backgrounds allows me to assist the students in not only clarifying their own positions on topics, but to think about how they and others might incorporate this knowledge into all of who they are. Many students have told me that they learn a great deal from listening to other students whose views on issues are different from theirs. For me, knowing when to shape discussion with my own input and when to allow students to learn from one another is something I'm still trying to refine.

Another way that I try to support students' full humanity in the class-room is by having occasional "life chats" with them. In one course, I spend about twenty minutes after each of three exam reviews discussing a topic that I feel will help them to think about their overall approach to life. Some topics that I find inspiring are everyday genius, effectiveness habits, and multiple intelligence. Sometimes I recommend books on these topics. One of my students last fall told me that after hearing about a book in my class, he had asked his parents to buy it for him for Christmas. It was *How to Think Like Leonardo Da Vinci* by Michael J. Gelb (1998), an excellent book about how ordinary people can develop well-rounded abilities in seven areas of genius. Gelb uses Da Vinci as an example of someone who exemplified genius in multiple areas. In other words, Da Vinci was a well-rounded gen-ius. Gelb's book gives useful exercises on how people can expand their strengths in seven major areas: curiosity, demonstration, sensation, open-ness, balance between art and science, corporality, and connection.

My passion for life leaks into my teaching. Students tend to note on my teaching evaluations how enthusiastic and caring I am. It seems that this sets them at ease and they learn to trust me. It also tends to make them more curious about *me* as a whole person. For instance, last semester in one class a student asked me if I had dressed up for Halloween. Instantly, it occurred to me to answer "yes," and tell them I went as a "transcendent spirit." I explained that I had not really dressed up but that I had gone to my meditation class. They were very curious and interested in this aspect of my life. I also told them that if I had dressed up, I probably would have worn my renaissance peasant outfit, which I got when I had my first teach-ing experience, teaching juggling! It seemed to amaze my students that I had once been a juggler and a mime in a theatre troupe. This type of occa-sional interaction gives me a chance to show the students my well-roundedness as well.

Because my courses deal with personal life issues of family and (in the past) death and dying, students seem to feel comfortable sharing challenges from those areas of their lives with me. This is especially true if an incident from that realm interferes with their regular participation in the course. I remember one year when I taught my course on death and dying. In the last week of this four-week intensive course, several of my 28 students had major issues that involved death or the danger of it. One student's father died suddenly, another had a friend who shot himself, and a third was assaulted outside his apartment. Two of these three students still made it to class, despite these incidents, and shared the details of what had happened with me. In my marriage and family class last semester, a student called to apologize for missing a class presentation and explained in detail that her aunt and uncle had been involved in a serious incident of domestic violence. We had just been discussing domestic violence in class! My course topics seem to open up the opportunity to talk about some of the major issues my students are dealing with, and I do not take that opportunity lightly. It gives me a chance to support them as the complex human beings that they are.

Activities outside the classroom provide additional opportunities for me to support students as holistic human beings. When students e-mail me or come to see me in my office, I try to recognize and support them as full human beings. I thank them for writing or coming by, and ask them about their lives in general and the challenges they face. Often discussions of missed classes or poor grades can lead to conversations about life priorities and personal troubles that students are facing. Without getting too excessive about it, I welcome these opportunities to know and support my students in the bigger picture of their overall lives. I have given support to students who were dealing with romantic break-ups, anxiety, hopelessness, uncertainty about their future, and sudden deaths of loved ones. It would be misleading to suggest that all my communications outside class with students is focused on life's serious challenges. I have also celebrated with students who told me about new occupational interests, successful interpersonal exchanges, increased clarity and self-esteem, and steps toward professionalism and achievement. As I take advantage of opportunities to connect and communicate with students, I keep in mind what a privilege it is to have a larger window into their lives and a chance to support them on their journeys.

Another out-of-the-classroom activity that I like to make available to the students is service learning. In my "Marriage and Family" course, the students have an option to visit local foster children and teenagers living in group homes. After a couple of visits, they work in groups to plan a party for these kids from troubled backgrounds. This project requires courage, as the students must deal with a certain degree of ambiguity (and sometimes discomfort) during their visits. They do not know what these children will be like or how they will respond to the students visiting them.

This service learning activity gives students the opportunity to bring their whole selves to a course project, and I believe for many of them it is the most memorable and profound activity for the course. It challenges them to work through their fears and to confront unexamined assumptions they have made about the world around them. The relevant aspect of it here is that it enables them to engage their whole beings into their learning—their intellectual and curious selves, their emotional and compassionate selves, their creative and fun selves, their social and personable selves, and so on.

Interacting with my students has caused me to develop broader connections with some of them, which I welcome. Several students have worked with me outside of class time to develop an "in-course honors" project related to the course. This cooperation helps me to get to know them better and opens other avenues as well. I have invited these honor students and other high achieving students to work with me as Undergraduate Teaching Assistants the following semester. In this capacity, they help me with grading, course coordination, and troubleshooting. I have tried to create this work with teaching assistants as a win-win situation, in which the students help me, and I help to coach them and support them toward their goals. Working with these students can also lead to other collaborative activities. One of my former teaching assistants (who had been one of my in-course honors students) became a resident assistant in one of the residence halls, and invited me to serve as a faculty mentor for her floor. This role involved participating in recreational and educational programming with a group of students across the entire school year. I enjoyed meeting Stephanie's residents, and I even taught some of them about meditation one evening as part of a stress-reduction program. One nice benefit to being a faculty mentor is that in this role I am encouraged to show more of my own holistic self. Social and recreational programs seem to bring that out a bit more than classroom teaching. However, the greatest reward from the faculty mentor activity for me has been the excuse to continue my relationship with Stephanie. After working so closely with her for multiple semesters, we have come to think of each other as friends.

There are other former students of mine with whom I have built friendships as well. One of these is my friend Eileen, whom I met in graduate school when I was a teaching assistant. Eileen and I kept up with each other as she graduated from college and went on to do graduate work in sociology. She later offered me the unusual opportunity of being the officiant at her wedding last year. I had not done this before and saw it as an incredible honor. What started out as a teacher-student relationship had flowered into a special friendship and role, in which I could celebrate Eileen and her fiancé Will as holistic individuals making a huge commitment to one another.

Other academic connections with students have led to additional opportunities to work with them on a more holistic level. One former student invited me to become the faculty advisor to her service club, Circle K International. I agreed to do this, and I have enjoyed seeing the enthusiastic members of this extracurricular club reach out to the community in service. Advising this club has also helped me to get to know the community better and to work with a group of students in a capacity broader than the usual academic one.

The third way in which my spirituality affects my teaching is central to how I arrived at teaching in the first place. I periodically remind myself how teaching fits into my sense of life purpose. I would encourage any teacher to think about this concept from time to time. This way of thinking goes back to the time period when I was finishing graduate school. I began to contemplate what was next. Should I teach college students? Create an outreach program for troubled youth? Join my brothers' rock and roll band? Unlike many of my peers, I did not assume that the next step had to be college teaching. Whatever came next, I decided I would link it to my life purpose. My sense of purpose makes priorities of personal growth, adventurous exploration, and service to humanity.

I got in touch with these areas of my own life purpose at a retreat on the subject in Sedona, Arizona. Pete A. Sanders Jr., author of the book *You Are Psychic* (1989), facilitated this retreat. We did a variety of exercises, some out in nature, to get in touch with our own unique sense of purpose for our lives. Neale Donald Walsch's (1995) *Conversations with God* books and retreats have also been intensely clarifying in this area. One retreat incident stands out very strongly in my mind. Neale asked us to write down what questions we felt we were facing in our lives at that time. Several of us shared our questions, which ranged from "how can I trust that I know what's best for me?" to "how can the drunk driver who killed my husband be brought to justice?" Neale encouraged us to consider that there were really just one or two central questions: "Who am I?" and "Who do I choose to be?" These questions helped me to think about who I was at the core of my being, and how I wanted to actively express that in the world. Another source that I have found helpful that relates specifically to teaching is Parker Palmer's (1997) book, *The Courage to Teach*. Palmer emphasizes the importance of teaching from who you are, and shows how that can be done to benefit students' learning.

Teaching is an act of service for me, one in which I can evolve personally and in an adventurous way. I seek to create opportunities for students to experience personal growth, adventure, and service as well. I use writing assignments, discussions, service learning, and group presentations to make these aspects available to my students.

The vantage point of life purpose frees me up to *choose* teaching as a way to live out my highest ideals. It also instills in me a sense of confidence that there are other things I could do that would also allow me to pursue the same big picture idea about my life. Awareness of this gave me confidence as I proceeded to apply for and accept a university teaching position. Right now, teaching is the occupational expression of my grandest vision of who I might be.

Sometimes I find opportunities to directly discuss life purpose issues with my students. One student came to me last semester, frustrated with trying to deal with manic depression. She was struggling to find a reason to want to live, and she asked me how I could be so positive about life. I shared with her that I had received many benefits from reading the *Conversations with God* books by Neale Donald Walsch (1995). She decided that she wanted to read these, and later she came back and shared with me her newly positive attitude and sense of purpose about her life. It was immensely gratifying to have this exchange with her, as I feel these types of core issues are the "stuff of life" that we all have to face on some level as human beings. Another example of directly discussing life purpose with students is an "in-course honors" student who is working with me this semester. She is trying to identify which type of graduate program is best for her. She was floundering a bit, unsure of what she really wanted to do. I asked her to step back and identify the life questions that seemed important to her. I asked her about her sense of life purpose and told her about mine. This exchange opened up a new line of discussion as we realized that multiple paths could allow her to actualize her dreams. We developed a plan in which she would make a list of a variety of occupations that would fit with her sense of purpose. This meeting was extremely rewarding for me and I think it was great for her, too.

In this chapter, I have discussed three ways in which spirituality relates to who I am and what I do as a teacher. These three approaches are meditating, supporting students as holistic human beings, and relating teaching to my sense of life purpose. Behind these actions are several beliefs. I believe in the value of a life balanced among intellectual, physical, emotional, spiritual, and creative pursuits. I believe that the more balanced I am among these, the more joy and insight I'll be able to bring to my teaching. I believe in the interconnectedness of all (human) beings. I believe that knowledge is not something I can give to others, but I can help others to develop an interest in acquiring it. I believe that teaching can facilitate the development of insight inside students and their teachers. These beliefs and the spiritual approaches I have described help me to keep a healthy perspective as I evolve as a college teacher.

References

Chopra, D. (1995). *The seven spiritual laws of success: A practical guide to the fulfillment of your dreams.* [Cassette recording.] San Rafael, CA: Amber-Allen Publishing.

Gelb, M. J. (1998). *How to think like Leonardo Da Vinci: Seven steps to genius every day.* New York: Dell Publishing.

Palmer, P. (1997). *The courage to teach: Exploring the inner landscape of a teacher's life.* San Francisco: Jossey-Bass.

Sanders, P. A., Jr. (1989). *You are psychic! An MIT-trained scientist's proven program for expanding your psychic powers.* New York: Ballantine Books.

Walsch, N. D. (1995). *Conversations with God: An uncommon dialogue.* New York: G. P. Putnam's Sons.

Learning Wisdom from the Jewish Oral Tradition

*Questions: When does a story begin? When does a heart open?
When does a story enter into the heart?*

Observing the Layers of Waves on the Sea

I was sitting on the beach in Ashdod, Israel, in January 2003, mesmerized by the waves with their white caps. Then I studied them more consciously trying to track their beginnings and endings. As in a dance, each wave began as a swelling—rose-crested with white foamy curlicues—folded into the Mediterranean Sea like milk foam dissolving into turquoise-colored cappuccino—waves infiltrating each other for centuries—then they lapped up to the shore. The shore is the end of one continent and the beginning of others, Asia melding with Africa and Europe.

More questions: When did the beginning begin? When are we ready to hear a story? Just as there are layers of waves, so too are there layers of openings of a story. One pebble can ripple out in circles and affect the whole body of water, drop by drop, inch by inch. Every being in this world is inspired and influenced by everything around and especially by the waves of our breath. Rami M. Shapiro captures this concept in his poem:

Nishmat [soul/breath] is the song of the wave
awakening to the ocean,
seeing that the wave is the ocean and the ocean the wave,

recognizing the interdependence of all things and
discovering the awesome wonder that is our reality. (Kol Haneshamah, p. 234)

So too can one breath, one whisper, one word, one silence affect the heart—but which word, which silence, which whisper? Which one begins the story? Which is the one that will open up the heart? What has the heart to do with teaching and learning? How does one teach from the heart?

Overview

In this essay I explore why it is crucial in education to address the heart. By illuminating the centrality of the heart in Judaism, the relationship of the teller and listener as a vibrant dyad becomes evident. It is when the heart is opened that true teaching and learning can take effect because then images remain and lessons become long-lasting. Furthermore, I examine the importance of story because the lessons transmitted through story can more effectively reach a person's heart. By telling stories the teacher does not present the lesson as a linear straightforward speech, but rather in an inspired, fluctuating, undulating, fluid manner, like the waves on the sea.

I view teaching as a sacred responsibility that affects another's consciousness, emotions, and knowledge. However, there still seems to be a dynamic mystery surrounding memory and learning processes in spite of numerous studies and research in these fields. However, I am convinced that in the relationship between teachers and students there is no substitute for the voice of a teacher telling stories. After all, the voice is produced by breath. In Latin, breath is *spiritus*, which can also mean inspiration, from *spirare*, to breathe. We can then see how breath/inspiration and voice are tied together in order to stimulate the faculties to a high level of feeling, and in this way, by telling and listening to stories, the storytelling teacher and listeners breathe together with their hearts beating in synchronicity.

A Cantor's Ritual Opening Prayer

To illustrate this idea I would like to tell you about a specific Jewish prayer that, when delivered from the heart, prepares congregants to enter into prayer. My father, Samuel E. Manchester, was a cantor, a singer of sacred liturgy in the synagogue. Every year on the Jewish New Year, Rosh

Hashannah, and Yom Kippur, the most sacred of the holy days—and only on these three days—the cantor chants a special prayer pleading with God to accept this leader's praying on behalf of the congregation. In other words, the cantor serves as a *Sheliakh Tzibur,* a messenger of the people. The ritual, which is being revived in many synagogues today, calls for the cantors to begin the prayer at the back of the synagogue and, while chanting, continue to walk to the *omed* (prayer stand). Only then would the formal prayer service "begin." (There are several "beginnings" here, too.) Just before this ritual, there would be a brief "intermission between acts" or between parts of the service. During this time, the congregation would take the moment to talk among themselves. Then, at the right time, my father would appear at the back of one aisle of the synagogue and wait: wait for the people to acknowledge his presence (through a rippling whisper of "Shhhhh, the cantor is ready to begin"). Very quickly the silence would become palpable. My father would also wait until he himself was ready to begin this most holy moment enwrapped with a mantle of responsibility. As the cantor began the first word of this prayer, "Heneni"—"Here I am"— he began to move slowly, haltingly, dramatically, chanting by heart and pleading with his whole heart, his voice coming from deep within him—at times both arms outstretched to the heavens. As he passed each aisle, the people began to enter into the solemnity of prayer, too. Finally, the cantor reached the place where his prayer book was already opened, ready to begin the main prayer service (*Mussaf*), together with the entire congregation. The journey up the aisle was a collective unifying experience, as though the cantor were lifting the disparate group of listeners to a higher spiritual level and bringing all the people with him to the sacred moment when they could all enter into prayer as one.

As a child witnessing this ritual, it was a powerful moment when I saw my father weep as he chanted in this heart-felt dramatic way. Although at that time I did not understand what was happening, it became a resonant memory for me, one that I have taken into my own storytelling approach.

The Heart in Judaism

Beginnings are a gateway to consciousness, understanding, knowledge, in other words, wisdom. In Judaism, the prayer book is designed with a sequence of prayers that serve as openings to prayer of various kinds. In storytelling, how does a storyteller begin or know when to begin? The best place to begin is with the heart.

The heart is so central that it embraces Judaism entirely: The last word of the Torah (the first five books of the Bible) is *Yisrael* (Israel) which ends in Hebrew with the letter *lamed*. The first word of the Torah is *Bereshit* (In the Beginning) which begins with the Hebrew letter *bet*. Together these two letters, *lamed* and *bet*, create the word *lev* which means "heart" in Hebrew. In Judaism, stories told from the heart work best in teaching long-lasting messages. As Rabbi Nahman of Bratzlav, the great eighteenth-century Hasidic master, taught: "Stories bypass the intellect and enter directly into the heart" (my paraphrase).

However, what happens when teachings do not enter directly into the heart? In Judaism's core declaration of one God, it states: "You shall take to heart these words that I command you this day." Another translation is: "These words, which I myself command you this day, are to be upon your heart." The rabbis interpret this as meaning that when a lesson is *upon the heart* or taken *to heart*, it is there ready to enter the *neshama* (soul). However, stories told from the heart and by heart (more on 'by heart' later) do more than touch us deeply, they also bring us to an ocean of wisdom and connection.

Little did I know that a story my mother had told me many times when I was a child would rest upon my heart until I was ready to apply its wisdom when I needed it most. It was a story about how to restrain my anger. Once there were a husband and wife and their baby son. As a Jew, the husband was forced to join the Russian Army and was sent far away. One night, after 25 years, the husband returned home. Through the slightly opened door he heard his wife talking with a man. Jealous with rage, the husband grabbed his revolver ready to shoot his wife's lover. Just as he was about to shoot, he heard the young man say, "Mama! Mama!" He realized that this was his own son, grown up, and he fell to his knees thankful that he had not shot his son. Whenever I lost my temper, my mother gave me this advice through this teaching tale she had heard from her mother. (In my research, I discovered a variant of this story in a thirteenth-century collection, Sefer Hasidim, by Reb Yehuda HaHasid.) One day, when my young daughter did something that made me lose my temper, my heart suddenly opened to that story. At that very moment, I hesitated and thankfully restrained my anger. Instead, I hugged her and spoke to her with loving words. We never know when a breath, a word, a story may be the vehicle that connects us to wisdom, healing, and reconciliation.

Heart as the Seat of Memory and Recollection in Torah

When we use the expression "to learn a story *by heart*," we usually mean to memorize it. When we recite a story by heart, we usually mean by rote or delivering a story out loud, memorized word for word, without necessarily having full comprehension. Rote involves unthinking repetition or mechanical routine. However, according to the Torah, the heart is considered the seat of memory and recollection "along with one's secrets" (Schroer & Staubli, 2001, p. 44). There is nothing routine about memory, and it certainly is fluid, much like the waves in the sea. So that when I use the term *by heart*, what I mean is that it comes from a deep place within us with bridges to associations, feelings, connections, and secrets—along with sense memories—that we make and keep in our hearts.

Interestingly, I found a rare definition of "rote" to mean also "the sound of surf breaking on the shore." If you listen carefully, that sound may seem to be repetitious, but, like all sounds of nature, each wave brings a different chord from a far away place deep in the ocean floor. In fact, some have posited that the waves have a language; we just do not yet have the ability to break their code.

Heart as the Seat of Wisdom in Talmud, Kabbalah, and Folklore

While I have already indicated that, according to biblical interpretation, memory is located in the human heart, the intellect or thought is placed in the heart as well. "In the Bible the heart is primarily the locus of reason and intelligence, of secret planning, deliberation, and decision" (Schroer & Staubli, 2001, p. 43). Thus, when King Solomon prays for and receives an understanding heart, "God gave him a heart of great wisdom, discernment, and breadth of understanding [heart] as vast as the sand on the seashore . . . He was wiser than anyone else. . ." (I Kings 4:19–33; cf. 3:12).

However, there are many complex discussions in the Talmud about the heart. Situated between the upper part of the body and the lower, the heart takes on a different interpretation in the rabbinic and kabbalistic traditions. As it states in *Mashmia Shalom:* "On a spiritual level we may say that the head is the seat of the intellect, wisdom, and knowledge of God. 'The spirit of the beast' is situated in the lower part. The moderator between the two extremes is the heart, which gives life to both parts" (Finkel, 1995, p. 158). In contrast to the western concept of the separation of the intellectual mind in the brain and the emotions in the heart, in Jewish tradition the heart is considered the center of the inner life. "In Kabbalah, God's heart corresponds to the *Sefirah* (divine emanation) of *Tiferet,* Beauty, at the center of the sefirotic tree. This aspect of God harmonizes and connects all the opposing divine energies into a loving unity" (Frankel & Teutsch, 1992, p. 75).

In Jewish folklore, too, the heart is recognized as a repository of wisdom and emotions, a combination of the cognitive and the affective. One of the major motifs in folk literature is "God wants the heart" (Motif: V 51.1). This comes from the saying, "Rakhmana lieba ba'ee" (God Wishes the Heart), which, according to folklorist Dov Noy, is based upon the Talmudic maxim in Sanhedrin 106b, which stems from I Samuel 17:7. In Psalms 116:6 there is also a reference to the simple man: "God guards the simple." In many of these folk stories a drought occurs in a certain place. After a time, a simple ignorant man is finally asked to pray for rain (usually because the rabbi has a dream that directs him to the simple man), then this simple man prays with his whole heart, although he does not know the correct words of prayer. Only then does God send the needed rain. It is the intentions or the intuitive wisdom of the simple man that reach God. In other words, it is not the formal representation of the normative religion that is heard, but rather the pleas of a uneducated man whose faith and deeds emanate from the heart (see Schram, 2000, pp. 49–53).

Stories Engage the Heart

Kieran Egan (1989) quotes Lucien Levi-Bruhl, who states that memory in oral cultures "is both very accurate and very emotional" (p. 457). Egan affirms that "The emotional coloring of events—or rather, the infusion of emotion into events—makes them more memorable. The technique that had developed in oral cultures for orienting the emotions with events was, once again, the story. In stories, narrators can direct the affective response of listeners to whichever elements they wish. Thus, in transmitting the lore of the culture through myth stories, this remarkable narrative device could be used to engage the emotional commitment of the listeners to the social group and to its customs and mores" (Egan, 1989, p. 457).

Whenever I tell the story of Joseph and his brothers (Genesis 37–50), there is an "infusion of emotion into events." Weeping is a main motif in the Joseph story, and perhaps that is why I am drawn to these episodes. Joseph, Jacob's most beloved son, was a dreamer and a dream interpreter. His ten older brothers were so jealous of Joseph, especially when Jacob gave him a "technicolor dream coat," that they conspired to throw him into a pit and then decided to sell him as a slave to Midianites on their way to Egypt. The brothers returned to their father but told him that Joseph had been killed by a wild beast, showing him the coat of many colors drenched in animal blood. Through a series of events, Joseph was brought to the pharaoh to interpret his dreams. Joseph foretold that there would be seven years of plenty and seven years of famine. When I tell about the seven years of famine, I tell how it was a time without rain, a time without tears, and a time when Joseph was alone without family and love, experiencing a sense of betrayal by those whom he trusted and loved. I want to reach the listeners not only with the narrative, but with the human emotions of the character to whom everyone can relate. I frame the story and interweave within the story related experiences from *midrash*—this term applies both to a method of interpreting Scripture to bring out lessons through stories or homilies and to a particular genre of rabbinic literature—as well as from my life so that Joseph becomes someone they care about.

Because of his wisdom and practical advice in preparing for the famine, Joseph became the Grand Vizier in Egypt. Due to the famine in the land of Canaan, Jacob was finally required to send his older sons to Egypt to buy grain. In the scene where Joseph sees his half-brothers, the brothers speak among themselves in Hebrew thinking that the Grand Vizier cannot understand them. They never imagine that he could be their brother Joseph. But when Joseph hears them express regret amongst themselves for what they had done to their brother Joseph, "He turned away from them and wept . . ." (Genesis 42:24). At this point, the listeners must sense Joseph's compassion for his brothers, rather than his wanting to seek revenge. The listeners internalize into their memory the powerful images of these brothers' peaceful reconciliation.

A major way that storytellers plant values and lessons is to be "in the moment" during the telling, no matter how many times they tell the same story. How is this goal accomplished? Once, Andres Segovia, the well-known Spanish classical guitarist, was interviewed by a reporter. The reporter asked the guitarist who was, at this time, in his 90s, "Surely you have played some pieces at almost every one of your many thousands of concerts. Tell me, don't you ever get bored?" And Segovia replied, "I never get bored because I am present at every note." I find this story inspirational because it teaches me two important lessons, that one has to stay in the moment to be able to enjoy even a much repeated piece to make it fresh and meaningful, and that one has to have an interplay with the music—never by rote—but rather note by note, or through a story image/word by image/word so that there is heart and passion in order to rediscover its power. This is the same lesson I learned with seeing/hearing/feeling/experiencing my father's concentration while he chanted the cantor's special prayer.

Through my story searching I have been fortunate to find many stories that I love and must share. Here is another example of how I teach from my heart. In "The Apple Tree's Discovery," a little apple tree, through every season, is envious of seeing the majestic oak trees with stars on their branches. The apple tree desires to have stars too. (Of course what the apple tree is seeing are the stars in the sky through the high-above oak branches.) Finally, in autumn, God causes a wind to blow and the apples fall, splitting open. The apple tree discovers that within each apple there is a star. While I am telling the end of this story, I cut open an apple, not by holding the apple with its stem up, but rather by turning it and cutting it on its side. When I hold up the two parts of the apple and show the star, I always hear a sudden intake of breath, an "Oh!" followed by smiles and laughter of joyful discovery. Once an elder came over to me and said, "I've lived 92 years and never knew an apple had a star inside. Thank you!" Children and adults alike are filled with wonder when they hear this story. Each time I tell it, I am there as the apple tree reaching for something outside of me, but, at the end, discovering anew that that "something" is within me. This is a valuable lesson to transmit, especially to young people. I have had people tell me they recall this story even eighteen years after I had told it to them (see a version of this story in Schram & Davis, 1995, pp. 1–4).

The Dynamic Flow Between Listening and Response

While the live voice and physical presence of a storyteller command attention, the storyteller also necessitates a response. As Ong states, "Narrative originality lodges not in making up new stories but in managing a particular interaction with this audience at this time—at every telling the story has to be introduced uniquely into a unique situation, for in oral cultures an audience must be brought to respond, often vigorously" (1982, pp. 41–42).

Response, in the case of a storytelling event, can be in the form of laughter, a knowing smile, a nod, a tear, a verbal response, a singing response, a response of a predetermined gesture, such as rhythmic clapping, and so forth. When listeners anticipate the response in an active manner, they actually enter into the storytelling experience as partners with the storyteller. Here, then, is a paradox: I tell you a story, but you are the storytellers.

Telling stories face to face is the most direct human interactive experience that creates rapport and draws people close. In this exchange, the storyteller and the story listener share their innermost feelings, thoughts, and values in a most entertaining way, through a story. A magic circle is drawn around the perimeter of the space incorporating the storyteller and the listeners. Walter Benjamin (1968) explains: "The storyteller takes what he tells from experience—his own or that reported by others, and he in turn makes it the experience of those who are listening to his tale" (p. 87).

The events of September 11, 2001, had a transforming impact on all of us in New York City, in America, and in the world. In the aftermath of this horror, one way to achieve the needed healing and renewed hope in humanity was to hear each other's stories and to tell each other our stories, personal tales, and folktales. One of the stories I found I was telling more often than many others was "Elijah's Mysterious Ways." This is a story that puts injustice and perplexing mysteries of life into a perspective, filling us with essential components for life, namely hope and spiritual uplift (for the story, see Schram, 1991, pp. 3–6).

First I frame the story with questions, such as "How do we keep our balance?" and "Why do awful things happen in the world, especially to good people?" When I was a child and would ask these puzzling questions, my father would reply, "Life is like a circle. We can't see the entire circle all at once. We can only see one arc at a time. We often don't know the reasons for what happens. We must be careful not to probe with too many questions, because if we ask too many questions and go too deeply, that can be dangerous." Then he would tell me the Elijah story. When I tell this story to my audiences, I recount what my father had told me. However, I also plant some of my own "secrets" within the story. For instance, when the good couple invites Elijah and his friend to eat with them, I add, "The wife said to the guests, 'Come and eat with us. When company comes it feels more like a banquet.'" (My mother often spoke these words to guests in our home.)

Near the end of the story, Elijah turns to his friend and gives him a new perspective to aid him when he sees an injustice happening to people who deserve better. In an early version I wrote, "And when you see a righteous person suffering, remember that he is being saved from something worse." At one telling, I saw a couple who had survived the Holocaust and I just could not complete the sentence the way I had written/rehearsed it. I realized, at that moment, that I did not fully believe that idea. So I said instead, ". . . because no one can understand all of God's ways." I have since revised it in one of my published versions and incorporate it in all my tellings of this story.

These secrets implanted into the narrative, such as a family saying, a family name given to a character, a detail of an object, and so forth, help me open my storehouse of memories, to see people and events that connect me to the story in special ways. When I can tell this story, no matter how often, I tell it by heart and with heart because of all the voices that resonate in me. Even though the listener may not know about these "secrets," nevertheless, the storyteller and the listener become partners in the experience and allow the creation of a new world in which they often experience deep feelings of emotion.

Listening is a concept central to Judaism. The keynote of all Judaism is the creed Sh'ma Yisrael (Deuteronomy 6:4), usually translated as "Hear O Israel," but better as "Listen O Israel." The reason for speaking these verses aloud is so that our own ears hear these words. In his essay, "The Storyteller's Prayer," Elie Wiesel (1987/1996) writes: "It is no accident that 'Shma Yisrael—Listen, O Israel' has become imperative in Judaism. God needs an audience. Thus, the quality of any exchange depends upon the listener" (p. xiv).

Judaism understands listening as a major component in the communication process. As Wiesel writes in the same essay, "Once I asked my own master, 'I understand why the *mitzvoth*, the laws, were so scrupulously transmitted from generation to generation, but why the *aggadot*? Why the legends?' And my master answered, 'They are important because they stress the importance of the listener'" (p. xiii). This shared experience between the teller and the listener creates a bond and an exchange that remains in the heart, the place of wisdom where cognition and affect combine.

Stories Reach Hearts

Stories answer best the "heart" questions: Who am I? Who are my people? By what values did they live? How should I live? How should I die? What are the legacies that I should transmit to the next generation? How do I become a *mensch*, a compassionate, resourceful, empathic, ethical, reaching-out-to-others kind of human being? How do we interact with other people?

Teachers who teach through stories need to tell them with their whole hearts, not just with emotion, but also with intellect. In that way, the stories are chosen wisely for those who need to hear that specific story and learn the wisdom embedded in the story. As Rav Samson Raphael Hirsch (1808–1888) interprets a line in the Book of Exodus 13:8, "And thou shall tell your son in that day," to mean that you must tell it right into him through the ears to penetrate the heart. Teachers need to tell stories from their hearts right into the hearts of their students—and with their whole hearts.

While formative stories are heard in the early years, they become transformative stories as we grow older. Wonder and memory, although relatively ethereal and ephemeral responses, can lead to more concrete and enduring behavior as a result of hearing culture-based stories. This is the learning and integration into our lives of the history of a people, its rituals, traditions, customs, warnings, and advice. This, in turn, can be put into observable practices. And these practices are part of us.

Proposal to Incorporate More Stories Into Teaching

I propose that we restore the dignity and worth of stories told in home, synagogue/church, school, and camp life. We can do this in two ways:

1. to have more educators (teachers, clergy, and parents) committed to in-corporate storytelling into their talks, sermons, discussions, lectures, life rituals;
2. to encourage students to tell stories in various settings.

I believe that teachers must not be "outside" of the lesson, but rather must share our own perspectives and passions (with a balance). In teaching, we need to pursue connections that link the teacher, the subject and the students. In an article, "The Heart of a Teacher: Identity and Integrity in Teaching," Parker J. Palmer (1997) writes: "We need to open a new frontier in our exploration of good teaching: the inner landscape of a teacher's life" (p. 15). This approach encourages teachers to include personal stories from the teacher's life, traditional folktales, sacred stories, as well as biographical narratives of great people. He continues: "Good teachers join self, subject, and students in the fabric of life because they teach from an integral and undivided self: they manifest in their own lives and evoke in their students, a 'capacity for connectedness'" (p. 16).

Palmer gives one example of a great mentor who taught the history of social thought. ". . . his classes were . . . permeated with a sense of connectedness and community . . . He told stories from the lives of great thinkers as well as explaining their ideas" (p. 16). In this instance, the stories are biographical narratives, but narratives nevertheless. We are always drawn into a told story and learn more beautifully from it.

Suggestions for Your Journey as a Storytelling Teacher

First of all, anyone involved with students of any age and in any capacity, must attend to the stories they recall from childhood and their responses to those stories. Certain key questions would be helpful to ascertain the types of stories and themes you are drawn to:

1. Make a list of stories you tell and underline those stories you love to tell often. Is there a reason you love to tell certain stories more than others? Why? When do you tell them? How/when did you yourself hear these stories? Is there a pattern of similar themes or characters between these stories?

2. Write out the earliest story you can remember that was told or read to you. If it is a story that can be found in a written source, do not go to that source until you have written it out to the best of your memory. Then you can try to make a comparison between your recalled version and that of the written story. This will add insights into the kind of person you are by noting what you remembered and also what you forgot to include or what you might have changed.

Second, start the journey to discover, choose, and learn many more stories. There is no shortcut method of doing this except by the pleasure and time needed to read stories. At the end of this essay, please refer to the annotated bibliography of titles of collections of Jewish stories, primarily folktales. When you find a story you especially like and need to tell, perhaps find or create other versions of that story so that you can find your own voice in the version that you tell. We often tell stories with gems of wisdom that we ourselves need to remember or learn.

Third, create a cross-listing of stories to find again when needed. The card file or computer file should contain the following information: title of story, title of book, author/editor, publisher, date, page number, source, country, theme, value, and moral/message, list of characters, places, any specific foods/important words or phrases, and a summary or sequence of the story in outline form. It is also useful to list the holidays or other occasions when this story might be used.

Fourth, introduce in your classroom, at the holiday table, or wherever you are with students, family and friends, the subject, theme, or character for which you have a "perfect" story so that you can create opportunities to tell the story you have practiced and are eager to share. Frame your story with a personal experience or questions related to the story theme, moral, value, or lesson so as to create anticipation in the listeners. Clergy can try to incorporate a parable, folktale, or personal story into almost every sermon. Camp counselors can work in tandem to tell stories that might also incorporate music. (For more on participatory storytelling, see Schram, 1994.)

Finally, in order to accomplish what I have suggested above, begin working on learning stories and telling them at every opportunity you can. Work on storytelling techniques, especially to concentrate on telling it "in the moment" and to be "present at every note." (See the Storytelling in Education Resources References at the end of this chapter.)

A Story of Trust and Heart Connections

Once there was a prince who began to act like a rooster. He took off all his clothes, stopped talking the human language, ate only the food on the floor, and happily crowed as he stayed under a table in his room. The physicians were unable to cure the prince of this "illusion" that he was a rooster.

One day a strange little man came to the palace promising to cure the prince of this mysterious illness, but only on condition that no one interfere with his treatment for a period of seven weeks. The king and queen agreed.

The first week, the strange little man observed the prince. On the second week, he took off all his clothes and jumped under the table with the prince, eating only the food on the floor too. With each passing week, the strange little man started wearing clothes, then eating food in dishes on the table, then walking straighter around the palace—and finally, teaching the prince that he had to 'pretend' to talk the human language and learn other types of human behavior—but that he could do all of this and still remain a rooster. Otherwise, he might end up as the main course on the holiday table.

And when, in time, the young prince became a great King ruling over the entire kingdom, no one besides himself knew that he was still a rooster. (See the full version of "The Rooster Who Would Be King" in Schram, 1987/1996, pp. 292–295)

This story, originally told by Reb Nahman of Bratzlav, the greatest of the Hasidic storytellers, is a "how-to-educate-a-person" tale. How to make a student into a *mensch* by going down to the level of students and bringing them up to a higher level. This story demonstrates the trust and the heart connection that must first be established between a teacher and students. This is what I learned to do in my storytelling from hearing my father chant the special cantor's prayer at the High Holy Day services. Not only do we have to have a communication with the story, but there must also be a mindful heartfelt connection between the storyteller and the listener.

In Psalm 92, the righteous are compared to a palm tree because the branches of a palm tree grow from its heart, unlike all other trees. This could be the metaphor for the way to teach from the heart. Teachers must first go within, connect personally with the story, and, in that way, tell the story from their hearts by reaching out to the hearts of others.

There are various relationships important in Jewish teaching: between the teacher and student; between the intellect and the emotion; between content/meaning and application. When the heart is present in the teaching exchange, especially through the medium of stories, then the lessons become transformed into deep-hearted wisdom ready to be drawn upon in life and brought to life through the breath and the voice.

References

Benjamin, W. (1968). The storyteller. In *Illuminations: Essays and reflections* (pp. 83–109). New York: Schocken Books.

Egan, K. (1989, February). Memory, imagination and learning: Connected by the story. *Phi Delta Kappan,* 70(6), 455–459.

Finkel, A. Y. (1995). *In my flesh I see God: A treasury of rabbinic insights about the human anatomy.* Northvale, NJ: Jason Aronson Inc.

Frankel, E., & Teutsch, B. P. (1992). *The encyclopedia of Jewish symbols.* Northvale, NJ: Jason Aronson.

Mashmia Shalom. (1969). Jerusalem: Amshinov Yeshiva, 160.

Ong, W. J. (1982). *Orality and literacy: The technologizing of the world.* New York: Routledge.

Palmer, P. J. (1997, November/December). The heart of a teacher: Identity and Integrity in teaching. *Change,* 15–21.

Schram, P. (1987/1996). *Jewish stories one generation tells another.* Northvale, NJ: Jason Aronson.

Schram, P. (1991). Elijah's mysterious ways. In *Tales of Elijah the Prophet* (pp. 3–6). Northvale, NJ: Jason Aronson Inc.

Schram, P. (1994). Participatory storytelling: A partnership between storyteller and listener. In *Tales as tools: The power of story in the classroom* (pp. 95–98). Jonesborough, TN: The National Storytelling Press.

Schram, P. (2000). Gates of tears. In *Stories within stories: From the Jewish oral Tradition* (pp. 49–53). Northvale, NJ: Jason Aronson.

Schram, P., & Davis, R. E. (1995). The Apple Tree's Discovery. In P. Schram (Ed.), *Chosen tales: Stories told by Jewish storytellers* (pp. 1–4). Northvale, NJ: Jason Aronson Inc.

Schroer, S., & Staubli, T. (2001). *Body symbolism in the Bible* (L. M. Maloney, Trans.). Collegeville, MN: The Liturgical Press.

Shapiro, Rami M. (1995). Nishmat is the song of the wave. In *Kol Haneshamah: Shabbat vehagim.* (2nd Edition). Wyncote, PA: Reconstructionist Press, 234.

Thompson, S. (1966). *Motif-Index of folk literature.* (Vols. 1–6). (Rev. ed.). Bloomington, IN: Indiana University Press.

Vitz, P. C. (1990, June). The use of stories in moral development: New psychological reasons for an old education method. *American Psychologist, 45*(6), 709–720.

Weiss, A. (1995). Black fire on white fire: The power of story. In Schram (Ed.), *Chosen tales: Stories told by Jewish storytellers* (pp. xv–xxxiii). Northvale, NJ: Jason Aronson.

Wiesel, E. (1987/1996). The storyteller's prayer. In P. Schram, *Jewish stories one generation tells another* (pp. xi–xvii). Northvale, NJ: Jason Aronson.

Storytelling in Education Resources

Barton, B. (2000). *Telling stories your way: Storytelling and reading aloud in the classroom.* Portland, ME: Stenhouse Publishers.

Booth, D., & Barton, B. (2000). *Story works: How teachers can use shared stories in the new curriculum.* Portland, ME: Stenhouse Publishers.

Bosma, B. (1992). *Fairy tales, fables, legends, and myths: Using folk literature in your classroom.* New York: Teachers College.

Collins, R., & Cooper, P. J. (1997). *The power of story: Teaching through storytelling.* Boston: Allyn and Bacon.

Egan, K. (1989). *Storytelling: An alternative approach to teaching and curriculum in the elementary school.* Chicago: University of Chicago Press.

Gillard, M. (1996). *Storyteller, storyteacher: Discovering the power of storytelling for teaching and living.* York, ME: Stenhouse Publishers.

Kinghorn, H. R., & Pelton, M. H. (1991). *Every child a storyteller: A handbook of ideas.* Englewood, CO: Teacher Ideas Press/Libraries Unlimited.

Lipman, D. (1995). *Storytelling games: Creative activities for language, communication, and composition across the curriculum.* Phoenix, AZ: Oryx Press.

Paley, V. G. (1990). *The boy who would be a helicopter: The uses of storytelling in the classroom.* Cambridge, MA: Harvard University Press.

Pellowski, A. (1990). *The world of storytelling: A practical guide to the origins, development, and applications of storytelling.* New York: H. W. Wilson.

Rosen, B. (1988). *And none of it was nonsense: The power of storytelling in school* Portsmouth, NJ: Heinemann Educational Books.

Tales as tools: The power of story in the classroom. (1994). Jonesborough, TN: The National Storytelling Press.

Trousdale, A. M., Woestehoff, S.A., & Schwartz, M. (Eds.). (1994). *Give a listen: Stories of storytelling in school.* Urbana, IL: National Council of Teachers of English.

Local Teaching

The Spirit of Place

"All politics is local." I have no idea if that famous statement is true, and I rather doubt any statement as sweeping can be true, but I do know that a great deal of teaching is local, and perhaps the best teaching always is. If I were to hazard my own grand generalization, I would say that teaching is always specific to its time and place. I cannot know if this is true for a certainty everywhere and always, but I do know that it has always been true in my experience, and experience is by what we have to test truth. To teach from the heart, from the whole of oneself, requires an active knowledge of the immediate here and now of the teaching situation and an openness to the unique and incommensurable particulars of one place at one time.

In the summer of 1988, I was finishing my doctoral studies in English at the University of Michigan. Jobs were especially scarce for English graduates that year, and the guidelines we received from the Careers Planning Office admonished us to be flexible about where we were willing to live and work if we hoped to secure placement. I took the advice to heart. My burgeoning student debt provided additional incentive for flexibility. I found an ad for a position at a community college in Laredo, Texas, that paid better than most and required only ABD ("all but dead" we used to say). I applied, accepted an offer, loaded my meagre graduate-student belongings in a U-Haul and headed south.

Ann Arbor, Michigan, and Laredo, Texas, are different places. In 1988, the average parental income of a student at the University of Michigan was approximately $85,000 dollars. Average adult income in Laredo that year was about $9000. South Texas has always been one of the poorest regions of the United States. With the exception of Appalachia, it may be the poorest. Ann Arbor, with the University of Michigan and various high-tech industries, is one of the wealthiest, although far from being the richest. The disparity in incomes and in privileges between Laredo and Ann Arbor had something to do with my decision to accept the position. I had been a poor student among rich ones for several years, and I wanted to turn away from that world thoroughly and for good. My supervisors were horrified by my choice, and their horror convinced me my choice was right.

I had accepted the Texas position for good reasons, but I knew nothing about teaching. During all my time at Michigan, teaching was never mentioned. Students of special promise were rewarded by not having to teach, and those who had to teach to pay their way looked for ways to minimize its interference with their research, which we all understood was the only road to advancement. Teaching was a necessary evil to be controlled and contained. "You exploit yourself or you exploit your students" was the mantra of my teaching assistant peers, and clearly the smart ones overcame their scruples and exploited their students. I never mastered the art of keeping students far enough away not to care about them, not to let them mess up my work. No matter how much I tried to resist them, I always ended up teaching for all I was worth.

What was I worth as a teacher when I came to Texas? Not much, I'm afraid. I had lots to learn, and what I needed to learn first was where I was. I have taught many different places since, but that is always the first lesson everywhere: learn where you are before you try to teach. My students at Laredo were different from me in important ways. Most spoke Spanish, I did not. Many were poor. I had come from a working-class background but never experienced serious want. Some of my students had. I was white. By white I mean *white*, my skin was pale, and my students' skin was dark, darker by genetics and darkened by the sun. The ethnic category of Hispanic embraces a broad range of peoples and pasts, and the overwhelming majority of my students were identified, according to census entries, as Hispanic. "Hispanic or White" the forms say, but "Hispanic" in Texas means mostly dark skinned, and the word that best described the ethnic heritage of my students, the word "mestizo" (or mixed) was not a census option.

Obviously, my students and I came from different worlds, and whatever I had to teach them about English literature and language would have to make sense in that place at that time. Many of my colleagues at the college disagreed. Like myself, quite a few of the teachers were new and from other parts of the country. They had been as flexible as I was when it came to moving but found it hard not to be rigid when they arrived. Some of the older teachers and administrators seemed to agree that our business was to teach a timeless and uniform "knowledge" that needed no adjustment for local conditions. The "authorities" were committed to what H. L. Goodall (1996) might characterize as the screaming paradox of an unconscious "Enlightenment project"—a "rational" model of learning that soon becomes supremely irrational in practice because it fails "to translate" (literally in my experience) "to locally sanctioned virtues" (p. 1).

The college's course catalogue was a telling example. The cover featured a young (white) couple dressed in athletic jackets walking arm-in-arm down a pathway with fall leaves skipping in the wind. I admired that cover. It represented an heroic effort to ignore the obvious and deny reality nearly psychotic in its thoroughness. Most of the year in Laredo is so searingly hot no one wears a jacket, and a common article of clothing for men is a short-sleeve shirt with an even hem worn outside the pants. The only trees on campus were ancient salt cedars with needles for leaves, and the nearest deciduous trees were about two hundred miles away. The catalogue might have served for a college in Northern Michigan, but it was a comic (one could argue sinister) distortion of South Texas.

Clearly, my colleagues and the college's administrators could not help me learn the things I needed to learn. I had to work primarily with my students. They would have to teach me how to teach them. We would have to be students together. Some of this work was done inside class, but much of it happened outside as well. The first thing to do was to start looking around. Walking through neighborhoods on hot afternoons was a start. Laredo is immediately across the border from Mexico. The narrow strip of the muddy Rio Grande separates Laredo from Nuevo Laredo, a city of several hundred thousand. Many of my colleagues at the college never crossed the border into Mexico. The heat, the crowds, the poverty, dismayed them, and it was dismaying. It was also, at times, wonderfully beautiful, but that was something one learned only after living there in patience for many days and months.

Perhaps the most prominent fact to recognize and understand was the land itself. In large urban environments it is increasingly difficult to have a sense of the sustaining land beneath the grid of streets and buildings, but the landscape of South Texas demands attention. Few places in North America are still as open as the brush lands of the Rio Grande valley. The land is fenced off and private, but much of it is still dedicated to pastoral or extractive industries. Consequently, it is largely unpopulated. For someone from the East or Midwest, the vistas are stunning and disorienting. One can drive a highway for hundreds of miles in almost any direction and see no structures larger than a shack, and most of them are few and far between. The arid West forces recognition of the particularity of place. Air conditioning pushes away the tremendous heat, but no technology or development has yet reduced the land to uniformity.

The violence of transformation that has made places like desert Phoenix humid from a concentration of backyard swimming pools has not reached South Texas and probably never will. Living night and day in a land so unmodified provides unmediated contact with the nonhuman order that one can so easily overlook in the reworked world of the urban east. The recalcitrance of the brush establishes and maintains the character of the region, and one's sense of the past seems sharpened in a space so resistant to change. Some of my northern colleagues lived in a kind of continuous terror of the heat and openness, but the land had to be learned and lived with before one would be entitled to teach. The landscape enforced a stillness commensurate with itself, and one came in contact with an environment where words were less sovereign than they seemed to be elsewhere.

So much was strange to me. In classroom discussions, my Hispanic students would often speak dismissively of "Mexicans" as backwards and lazy. I was taken aback by the casual racism and (as it seemed to me) the contradiction. Clearly, for many of my students, nationality was far more significant than ethnicity, or nationality was itself, by some strange process, reinterpreted as ethnicity. The narrow strip of the Rio Grande changed one irrevocably. Their parents may have come from Mexico, but my students were now Americans, a new species created by a change in geography. I wondered if my immigrant Irish or German ancestors had talked this way about their countrymen back in Ireland or Germany. They may have, and I had simply forgotten their immigrant passions and angers. A great deal was called into question in this border country between the United States and Mexico, and I was one of the things that was increasingly questionable.

My experience as a teacher in Laredo also changed how I now understand my own experience as a student. In both undergraduate and graduate programs at the University of Michigan, I remembered how few of my teachers were from Michigan or the Midwest. Most were from prestigious universities in the coastal east or west. Many of my instructors knew nothing about the state they taught in outside the financially upscale Ann Arbor. They were more likely to visit Italy any given week than Detroit, to say nothing of the rural towns to the south and west of the university. The land around them, and the history of that land, even the economic and social life of the people in that land, meant nothing to them. The university was a kind of geometric point in an atemporal abstract space of knowledge entirely divorced from the trivial accidents of "regional" history and geography. My teachers did not need to know where they were. They were island inhabitants of a region of wealth and privilege who knew the shortest routes to the airport.

I wondered if I appeared that way to my students in Laredo. I am sure I did at first, and I could have gone on in that way to the end of my stay. Many of my colleagues served their terms as visitors from another planet always looking away to Austin, at least, if not to Boston, Cambridge, or Ithaca. I did not want to be another version, on a smaller scale, of the airplane-teacher waiting for the next flight out. I had experienced such teaching and found it deadly, a deracinated professionalism that substituted institutionalism and bureaucracy for the life and breath of living persons in the here and now. Ivan Illich (1970) has talked about the "hidden agenda" of institutionalized teaching, which conveys a consistent message of institutional dominance through every content of instruction. I did not want to fill the role of an emissary from this system for students who clearly wanted something else.

I allowed students to befriend me. I let them "waste my time." I worried less about maintaining "professional distance" and started asking questions. I learned about the system of spiritual faith healing in South Texas known as "curanderismo," and my students were surprised that I wanted to learn from them. I learned about language, about the patois spoken in South Texas that is neither English nor Spanish, but a mixture of the two called TexMex, which is often scorned by both English and Spanish speakers in the linguistic centres of Mexico and the United States. I learned about the complex history of race and racism along the border. The spirit of a place is also the history of a place. The immediate here and now is also the persistence of the past, and learning about my students in the present also meant learning about the history of the region.

The history of South Texas is often a record of brutalities and violence, of racially motivated murder and reprisals. The popular history of the state glosses the terrors that produced the present border. Many of my students knew this and could provide accounts from family history of the alternating killing and cooperation that existed between the different ethnic communities of the area. Personal history of this kind could be a source to explore in our writing and reading in class, but to introduce it, I had to let my students speak as authorities because I was not in the know as they were and I never could be. What I could do is show them that their local knowledge was important and honored, that it contributed to what they were assigned to learn in class. Their personal history was recognized as real and meaningful, and what I could give was the recognition of one who did not know but was willing to learn. My learning was the lesson I taught.

I allowed my students to make fun of and even express their contempt for what we were assigned to learn. In an introductory literature course, we were required to read *Beowulf*. On the first day, when I began to mention some of the major characters, several students began laughing. What was funny, I wondered. After considerable hesitation, one student volunteered, "the names are funny." Why were they especially funny? In a moment I understood. In Spanish, the "h" is generally unsounded, and Germanic names like Hengest, Hrothgar, and Hygelac, with their aggressively sounded aspirant, would sound more than ordinarily odd. My own name (Hoth) had often presented a problem to my students for this reason, and for years I had become accustomed to answering to the pronunciation of my name as "Ot." In a moment's inspiration, I asked, "what about your names? Aren't they pretty funny? Zuniga? Villarreal? Sound pretty funny to me." My students were stunned. "These are my people," I continued. "Hrothgar, Hengest, Hoth, you're talking about my name when you talk about these funny names." In one of those moments that are magical, a student responded, "Your name *is* funny." Everyone (myself included) laughed. That began a very useful discussion about language and names and ethnicity that was more pertinent to the tensions and themes of *Beowulf*, with its conflicts between Geats and Danes, than most of the scholarly chat I have read about it in academic periodicals.

My experience in Laredo can be given theoretical description. Mary Louise Pratt (1992) has written about "contact zones," places where different cultures meet and where they negotiate or contest conflicting values and structures. Postcolonialists such Homi K Bhabha (1994) talk about "hybridity," the intermingling of disparate systems in the breakdown of colonial hierarchies. These theoretical descriptions are apt and accurate as far as they go, but the experience of place is not a theoretical description. To learn the realities of one time and one place, one has to resist generalizations, the theoretical "knowledge" that can flatten or distort experience by sacrificing "detail" to "mastery." Postcolonial theorizing often becomes another form of colonization, turning raw local life into theoretical product for academic/colonial markets in major intellectual capitals. The humility of conscious ignorance is a precondition of learning deeply about what we see and hear before us. If we want to know a place in its particularity and the people who live there, we must be willing to forget our professional languages and categories. We must be willing to speak the language we encounter before trying to translate it or speak over it. In my case, this meant returning to infancy in attempting to learn Spanish moment-by-moment and day-by-day as my students taught me.

Being attentive to the spirit of place as a foundation for learning and teaching has led me to reflect more deeply on the meaning of the community college in higher education. Community colleges were commonly called junior colleges in the past, and it is safe to say that many still see them as inferior substitutes for or remedial avenues to a university education. That is how I thought about them at first. That is how most of my colleagues think about them still. Now, I think differently. The community college may be an opportunity for learning and teaching that attends to the humble immediacy of people living together in a given region. It may not be a substitute for a university education, but it is certainly a corrective. The poverty of abstraction and disconnection that afflicts so much higher education may be easier to address, and perhaps redress, in the less prominent institutions of the community college system.

Teaching that is attentive to the here and now of one place and one time can exist wherever teaching occurs, provided one is willing to care about the merely local and immediate. No institution exists without its history and its implication in the conditions of its place, although it is often easy to ignore these, and some institutions encourage, even enforce, this selective attention. The concept of higher education in North America is wedded to the notion of power and prestige defined as access to material and cultural products produced in the urban centres. From this perspective, anywhere away from a few major universities is a wilderness of ordinary life. Teaching locally means turning away from this centralizing and devaluing control.

In the end, the surest way to achieve local awareness is to accept one's limitations and insignificance by recognizing the here and now of contingency and circumstance. So many different possibilities of human life exist and have existed, and for most human beings, the possibilities remain and are realized locally and regionally. Even for many cities and towns in North America, life is still largely a matter of neighborhoods and districts. We tend to suggest that important teaching occurs away from these places in central institutions endowed with ample capital, and certainly teaching that attracts attention and funding does almost always occur a long way off from most people's local world, but good teaching takes place wherever a teacher and student are placed, especially whenever they are both attentive to the meaningfulness of the place they are together.

Much has changed in Laredo since my stay there years ago. The homogenizing highway architecture of middle America has begun to transform the barrios and colonias of the older city, but the surrounding land is largely unchanged, and perhaps unchangeable. I return there infrequently to visit friends and to remember the strangeness of my first arrival and all it taught me about myself and about teaching. The tangible and yet intangible particularity of the place remains a guide for me now in any place, a reminder that whatever appears "general" and "standard" is always a constructed illusion, a form of forgetting the spirit.

References

Bhabha, H. K. (1994). *The location of culture*. London: Routledge.

Goodall, H. L., Jr. (1996). *Divine signs: Connecting spirit to community*. Carbondale, IL: Southern Illinois University Press.

Illich, I. (1970). *Deschooling society*. New York: Harper & Row.

Pratt, M. L. (1992). *Imperial eyes: Travel writing and transculturation*. London: Routledge.

The Spirit of the Real in Theatre Education

A Real Night(mare) in Regina

As a teacher of theatre, I find that when teaching, theatre, and the relationship of these two practices touch reality, there is an engagement with spirit in the very heart of subjectivity. Inviting spirit into my pedagogical practice is an invitation to recover the lived experience of both teacher and student. Fleshing out the felt subtleties of our own subjectivities in the real spaces of experience, we touch the unknown, the unpredictable, the mysteries of the moment. As we are stirred to new understandings, it is in the dance between self, other, and environment that we awaken the experience of spirit. In this chapter I explore my work with students in site-specific theatre. In leaving the traditional classroom we embark on a journey of interrelation with site and other that opens us to the wonder of the real.

In January 2000, I took a position in the Theatre Department of the University of Regina. Not sure if I would stay there, and not keen on the idea of moving my family across Saskatchewan in the middle of winter, I decided to live there on my own for the first term and get my bearings. My wife and children were a five-hour drive away, so I planned to rent a room and live in Regina during the week, and travel to my family on weekends. Deciding that my best option was to find a room in a house downtown, I moved into a nice old house in the city's Cathedral district. Having moved from Lloydminster, a small city with little architecture predating 1960, it was a pleasure to be living in a place with lovely old buildings. Regina has been graced by talented architects, and its relatively slow economy (as compared with cities such as Calgary or Edmonton) has meant that old buildings have been left standing, not torn down to create the appearance of progress. Even the house in which I rented a room was at least 70 years old, and I could see traces of its history every time I climbed the staircase and saw the marks of past inhabitants; when I slept in my room and could hear how the building "spoke" through its structure, the creaks and squeaks in response to its other occupants, and the rumbles and vibrations through pipes and ducts.

By my third night, I was becoming pretty well acquainted with my place in this house. As I unpacked my things, gradually my room was reflecting my presence. I was able to cook, eat, and sleep comfortably, but I had no phone service, nor had I become acquainted with any of my housemates. Keen to get my courses prepared and underway at the university, I was only home at night during this first week. On this particular night I came home at about 8:00 p.m., and while eating my dinner noticed for the first time the sounds of music and conversation coming from my neighbour. I appreciated these sounds of other housemates, of company, as I reflected on my own state of separation from my family. These vibes of a good time lulled me to sleep through the wall. However, this good vibe went horribly wrong as I awoke to sounds of violence at about 2:30 a.m. Slowly realizing these sounds were not a nightmare, I lay awake in a state of paralyzed self-debate about what could be happening and what I should do. I could hear the sounds of a woman's voice pleading, the sounds of a man's voice accusing, the thuds and other noises of impact that punctuated the voices. I had no phone for calling the police, and for what seemed like hours I felt I could not leave my bed—despite its close proximity to the wall through which the violence reverberated. In this moment I was struck by the "unreal" reality of what I was experiencing. I was caught in a kind of purgatory of the real—between the reality of physical violence and my peculiar experience of it, through a wall, half-awake and in a still unfamiliar room. This purgatory lasted a couple of hours until someone else in the house had the sense to call the police. Then came sounds of the aftermath, the heavy footfalls of the police, the muffled crying, the sounds of detective work, and finally an opportunity to make a statement—with a promise of a date in court as a "witness" to what had happened that night.

It was hard to live in this house after what had happened. I managed to stay for another couple of weeks, while other arrangements were made. The house was haunted with the reverberations of the violence of the attack. The landlady, away the night of the attack but with the best intentions, spoke about some kind of ritual of cleansing the house of the bad aura from the event, a kind of exorcism of the residual leftover of the experience for all of us who had endured it. While my landlady's intentions seemed like a positive step toward recovery of the situation, I wondered how helpful this would be for me. The anguish and shame that permeated the house was at once palpable and precarious. Attempts to identify the effect of my experience somehow failed, or existed in shadow, dissolving as soon as I tried to grasp it. I did not have nightmares of the event; however, the experience of just being in my room was changed forever, and just the act of going to bed was unsettling. The ground of my subjectivity had shifted, was permeated with the resonances of this event. In some respects it was like a rite of passage into a new order of being. I wondered how this experience might mark a shift in my pedagogical practice. In discussing my situation with colleagues, many reflected upon how the traumatic aftershock of this event seemed like a haunting. One colleague, quite interested in ghosts and paranormal activity, suggested that the negative energy left behind from a traumatic event—often ending in death—was the source of most haunting. Moreover, he suggested that the neighborhood I lived in, replete with old houses, was a center of paranormal activity in Regina.

Sadly, this negative early experience of living in Regina reaffirmed many of the stereotypes the city endures from the perspective of people living in other parts of Saskatchewan, or even in other parts of western Canada. Before going, I was warned that Regina is the West's crime capital, and that I would be at great risk there. There were plenty of stories about violent incidents that haunted my imagination of this city. I had to admit that I was not accustomed to witnessing such violence so close to—indeed, within—my home. However, under the spell of the positive potential of a new job, and my growing fascination with environmental theatre practices, I was able to draw a kind of inspiration from this event. My experience of this night seemed to offer insight into at least four areas of concern for me as a teacher and practitioner of theatre. The first had to do with the role of the witness in the context of site-specific theatre practices. The second had to do with the site of the event itself, and how events can trigger hauntings; perhaps not unlike certain learning experiences that are difficult to face, and yet they remain with you for the rest of your life. The third was how the dramaturgical weave of the first two, site and witness, might give rise to an experience that challenges how we define the real as either a referent or a signifier of theatrical practices. The fourth concerned dramaturgy, and how its applied practices, as taught in university programs and in the profession, made it an attractive part of theatre practice and education to begin experimenting with the above innovations in theatrical form. In my first few classes of teaching a production dramaturgy course at the University of Regina, it seemed the students were haunted by some of these concerns as well.

A Dramaturgy Dream at the University of Regina

As is the case with any new faculty, there is always a feeling of "filling the shoes" of your predecessor in your department. Your syllabus, your first few classes, and your whole approach to the course is without doubt haunted by the approach of your predecessor. In the production dramaturgy class the influence of the previous teacher was pronounced. I figured that the best way to deal with this situation was to face it head-on and actively solicit my students' perceptions about the course. As it turned out, their expectations were entirely in keeping with my predecessor's approach. For the most part, my students were concerned about dramaturgy being long on research and paperwork while being short on creativity and practical application. Within the walls of academia their spirits had been deadened, resigned to performances of paper and pen. As a way of demonstrating my faith in their spontaneous, creative abilities, I went through an imaging exercise with them. When asked to create a tableau of a "nightmare dramaturgy experience" they repeatedly produced images of being buried in paperwork; of researchers banished to the library, far from the creative process on the stage; of the tokenism often given to contextual research in the production process; and overwhelmingly I saw images of isolation. By contrast, their images of a "dream dramaturgy experience" were replete with the energy of creativity, collectivity, and projects that were relevant to their lives and to their experience of living in Regina. Through imaging we crossed a threshold to an imaginary world—a world filled with the wonder of the real. My students' dream images featured dramaturges at the center of the creative process of making a performance, and the role of the dramaturge appeared to be redefining the process of theatre creation. Here theatre looked more like the birth of a child, a rave, or a party. It was here that the spirit of my students and our creative endeavours as co-participants in engaging the spirit of the real first became palpable. Interestingly, none of these images appeared to be happening on a theatre's stage.

This flowering of imagery in the classroom, coming from students who feared that it was their destiny to endure a production dramaturgy class full of assignments fated only for my desk and evaluation, offered me insight not unlike that of the incident in my rooming house. In terms of the profession, I thought, dramaturgy need not be stuck in "a little room" of conventional usage, essentially terrified of what lay beyond these walls yet representing the stimuli of this world within the comfortable confines of a page or stage. Perhaps dramaturgical strategies might be utilized to creatively engage with real experiences that, although often ineffable and beyond symbolization, are revealed to haunt the symbolic order of the purpose-built room. Indeed, if a majority of professional theatre has become stuck in purpose-built spaces, obviously it is because there is great benefit in being there. Many professional theatres across Canada boast state-of-the-art lighting and sound systems. These facilities offer the best equipment for realizing the dreams of theatre artists—or do they? Theatre spaces seemed conspicuously absent from my students' dreams of theatre creation, so I began to think carefully about the link between dramaturgy, dreams, and the spaces of theatre creation. After all, I wanted to find a way to realize my students' dreams, to awaken the spirit of our practice.

The Form of Our Dreams and the Form of Our Theatre

In considering the relationship between dreams and theatre, it strikes me that both provide a particular space and time of speculation. Each offers a form of being in which we may be permitted to explore our desires and fears, our conflicts and our pleasures. I think it can be said that the theatre is a particular form of thinking, made possible by the conditions of theatrical representation. As Freud (1977) suggests, "dreams are a particular form of thinking, made possible by the conditions of the state of sleep. It is the dream-work which creates this form" (p. 650). Perhaps the "dream-work," the praxis of dreaming, is where education comes in, or at least the process of analysis. In terms of our experience of dreams or, as I would like to suggest, theatre and theatre education, two questions arise: First, as a particular way of thinking, why has theatre taken on certain forms, for example, a proscenium arch, a three-act structure, or a naturalistic staging? Why is the "essence" in the "work" or form of the dream and not as we might expect in its content? Moreover, in terms of education, similar questions arise concerning the forms of pedagogy, wherein content is given a good deal of consideration, but the forms in which this content is experienced and worked on by students are too often taken for granted. If I am to teach from the heart, it is the "taken for granted" that needs to be challenged. Stepping beyond the classroom walls, the classroom ruled primarily by considerations of content encourages the revitalization of relationship between student, teacher, and environment at the very core of inspired teaching.

A Trinity of Creation for Site-Specific Theatre: The Host/ The Ghost/The Witness

Drawing from personal experience and my growing understanding of Regina as a context for professional theatre and the work of my students, I developed a term assignment for my production dramaturgy class based on the following criteria. First, I wanted the class to explore the creative possibilities of dramaturgy. As an inspiration, I wanted them to explore a resource—something material, tangible, and simple. However, I felt it should be something that haunted them, even scared them a bit, or perhaps in some way it held a mystery for them. Second, while the work of dramaturges is often multifaceted, and therefore difficult to define, conventionally dramaturgical training has involved the research and presentation of historical materials to assist the actors, director, and designer in the development of a production. With this project, students were given the chance to move beyond standard approaches to dramaturgical practice in a couple of significant ways. Students were to research and develop material that they would, themselves, see through to performance. The performance would be written, directed, and performed collectively by the students. I wanted to encourage them to be theatre artists, and avoid the pitfalls of a "dramaturgy ghetto." I asked my students to research and prepare a performance based on a specific historical building in the city. In this case, their work would be devoted to a real, particular site of Regina's history, not just a fictional environment existing only on the stage of a theatre. I wanted them to consider the political and aesthetic implications of moving theatre practices out of theatres and into real, inhabited spaces in the community. Through this process, students were encouraged to consider broad questions concerning the place of theatre in relation to the community's history, architecture, and urban geography—and to consider these elements alongside their own collective and personal experience of place.

Reflecting on the parallels that had been drawn between my rooming house experience and haunting, I decided the resource should be a building in the city that is reputedly haunted. The choice of a haunted building as a resource for theatre creation seemed to effectively fulfil all of the criteria needed. It especially balanced the need for something straightforward—a building, in a sense an object that in essence we could all agree was just that, a building—and yet its haunting withheld a certain mystery. Above all, this assignment would also move the class and myself toward a better understanding of the role played by dramaturgy in site-specific theatre. It has been my experience in creating theatre in site-specific locations that perhaps the greatest benefit of the work is how it engages with a particular place that exists as an entirely independent entity from its use for theatre. I was also interested in exploring the kinds of engagement that might be possible between students and the real environments of their community.

Theatre designer Cliff McLucas (of the Welsh company Brith Gof) began to characterize his site specific theatre designs in terms of a "trinity of creation" wherein "The Place (the Host), The Performance (The Ghost) and The Public (The Witness) create a composite that becomes what is known as the 'work'" (McLucas 1993, p. 2). I borrowed and adapted McLucas's form of theatre creation and, with some alterations, used it as the model followed by my students. The dramaturgy assignment, entitled *The Host / The Ghost / The Witness,* had its final presentations during the week of April 2 to April 8, 2000, consisting of four performances which occurred around Regina, each offering an animation of a particular haunted, historical site in the city.

The four sites chosen included the Assiniboia Club, the city's oldest gentleman's club, part of which was recently converted into Danbry's, an upscale restaurant. This location was reputedly haunted by a young woman named Charity, who was believed to be a prostitute murdered in one of the private bedrooms of the club in the 1940s. The research on this site was impressive, including 16 interviews with former members and employees of the club and current employees of the restaurant; intriguing archival information that clearly indicated "an incident" involving a club member and this individual's subsequent dismissal; as well as a spiritual mapping done by a local specialist in this area of paranormal cartography. A downtown tavern called Bart's on Broad featured furnishings bought at auction that had come from saloons across the North American West. This project animated the various stories of hauntings that emanated from a bar and booth with bullet holes from a famous shootout involving Billy the Kid, a stained-glass window from the unhappy home of newlyweds who committed suicide, and a ceiling fan system from a bank in Cleveland that featured one of the bloodiest robbery shootouts in that city's history. Here was a collage of performed animations that cleverly tied all of these objects and their hauntings of misfortune into the performances of several lost souls who had finally found refuge in this tavern.

The dome of the provincial legislature building was also a site. Completed in 1913, this magnificent structure was open to the public because a viewing deck at its top featured the best view in southern Saskatchewan. Unfortunately this dome was closed to the public in 1967 because in that year Lawrence Hall, a local fire fighter suffering from schizophrenia, threw himself off the top of the dome and died. Curiously, the provincial records indicate that Hall had thrown himself off the building twice previously that year, and the site was finally closed to public access in part because of the failure of the Legislature staff to prevent his death. In keeping with the multiple personalities of his mental illness, legend has it that Hall was a master of disguises. In addition to the folklore surrounding Lawrence Hall, the students who worked in this site were also blessed with a wonderful archive of stories. Inside the dome, traversing its inner wall was a staircase along which had been scratched, stencilled, and inked the most interesting graffiti—hundreds of passages, poems, stories, and signatures—written on the wall along the ten-story climb toward the lookout deck at the top of the dome.

The last site chosen was 1800 College Avenue, which in the spring of 2000 was the home of Magellan's Global Coffee House. This "troubled house" of Regina's history became the focus of research and further performances that extended beyond this dramaturgy class because its owners were willing supporters of this work, and the heritage of this house—haunted and otherwise—was important to many in the community.

1800 **Confessions Avenue**

The production entitled *1800 Confessions Avenue* arose in part out of the site-specific dramaturgy project "The Host/The Ghost/The Witness" involving students Jill Wilton, Glenda Whalen, Tom Swanson, and Holly McLean, who developed a performance at 1800 College Avenue, and in part out of a directed studies class in site-specific performance involving students David McBride, Derek Porter and Glenda Whalen, who further developed the historical research of the site and techniques used in the performances of *1800 Confessions Avenue*. The fact that these students chose to develop their work in the first class in this second course speaks to the quality of their engagement with this dramaturgical project. Their commitment, the long hours of writing, staging and performance, was a testament to the heart of our learning and teaching practice. Something of our spirits had been touched in this process. In the following analysis, I want to establish how this method of developing theatre went a long way toward realizing the dramaturgical dreams of the students who created this work; that is, the creative process described below grew from a center of dramaturgical innovation, and this innovation grew through the students as it was their writing, acting, and design which brought their own research to practice in performance. The spirit and dedication they brought to this work was inspiring, and in a manner of speaking, it haunts me to this day.

The McKillop family built the house at 1800 College Avenue in 1911 but, due to financial troubles, were forced to sell it after only 11 years. For the next 45 years the Sneath family resided there; then the house was sold to a photographer as a site for business, and over the next 25 years changed ownership ten times. In my student's research, the story of Rose McKillop was by far the most popular. Through interviews and research into local archives, it was discovered that the house was actually built for Rose McKillop, and the traumatic event of losing her beloved house was public knowledge. Indeed, the story of how she ran from the house's back door—clutching her favourite vase in one hand and a child in the other while the creditors from the North American Life Assurance Company were coming through the front door to repossess the property—is often repeated in interviews with people who knew the family. From the time the McKillops lost the house, Rose apparently spent the rest of her life yearning to live there again. In the last few years of her life, she would often pack up the things from her room in her seniors' residence and to be found later in the day out in front of "her stone house" (Whalen 2000, p. 32) and ready to move back in. Joseph Thauberger, the first owner to use the building as a business, bought 1800 College Avenue in the spring of 1974. Rose McKillop died in April of that year. Thauberger was the first occupant to say that the house was haunted. Over the course of the next 26 years the building has had many occupants, all running businesses, and all with memories of ghosts. Usually the stories revolve around the image of an elderly woman or a woman's voice heard singing in the stairwell. There are also accounts of men arguing in the dining room, or of a cold, shadowy presence in the main floor room that was once used as an office.

Despite the multiple occupancy, the home's main floor with hardwood trim—French doors, fireplace facades, beams, window frames, and stairwell—has remained in remarkably good, original condition. The second and third floors, however, have been ruthlessly gutted, altered, and for the most part left bare by recent owners. This open space, with its scars, cavities, and traces of previous occupants, offered many opportunities for narrative and performance. The production of *1800 Confessions Avenue* was able to make good use of the various stories, traces, and scars of memory existing in a site with a history of "particular" uses other than theatre.

Real architectural sites encourage the practitioner to think and create in three and four dimensions. This has major implications for the concepts and practices at the heart of theatre. It may rewrite or problematize the nature of the relationships between all components of the event: between spectator as individual and spectators as a group, between spectator as individual and performer, between spectator as a group and performer, between performer and performer, between performer and architecture, and so on. In *1800 Confessions Avenue* the spectators began the performance seated in the main room of the coffee house that was once the living room and dining room, but they were soon required to follow the event into other rooms, upstairs, and into the various recesses of the house. In this respect the spectators share in the performers' exploration and discovery of the site in the most tactile way: through the sense of smell and touch as well as sight and sound. Moreover, in such an environment, performer and spectator alike discover that beyond the basic performative means of gesture and kinesics, the whole performance experience is empowered by proxemics—the distances between people—and haptics, the touch of self and others.

A wide range of narratives was created and culled for *1800 Confessions Avenue*. Beginning with historical facts about the building and its many inhabitants, we devised narratives, ballads, and physical scores around the archetype of "family" that existed in the house. Much of this work began with a basis in research, but soon it took on fabrication based more in the personal experiences of the performers than on found history. For example, the performance began with a chorus of confessional texts ranging from straight information about the house and its inhabitants to fantastical deeds, activities, and personal information that could not possibly have any direct relation to the house.

The fantastical departure from historical fact seemed to evolve organically for the students as their research inspired a fragmented narrative of exploration. They endeavoured to create an experience that might better be described as the mythologies, shadows, or ghosts of the factual history of this particular house. In exploring 1800 College Avenue, the ensemble of performers became *mediums* to experiences that were embedded in the house. While some of these experiences were set in actual history, more often they were a part of a different truth we felt the house must confess. As 1800 College Avenue became *1800 Confession Avenue*, the audience witnessed a history more deeply embedded in the psyche—to the mythical, the personal, and the imaginary.

Early in the performance—after the performers have offered their confessions, establishing their struggle to fully inhabit the text of this house—the audience is witness to a sequence of monologues, creating the different perspectives of the "family" they are about to follow throughout this house. David McBride performs the "son," and while sitting at one of the coffee house tables placed in the dining room, he recounts a memory of a dinner long ago. He has burnt himself on one of the dishes and says:

> It burns my hand, and I yank it back and then sit there holding my hand out for my mom to look at. She's concerned. But my dad, he's watching the whole thing while he's eating his calamari, and he's almost choking with laughter at me touching the skillet. There's this thing with his lip when he laughs. My sister always puts her hands over her ears. "Boy, that's a whole little character study of you right there," he laughs. Big red loud laugh. My hand is red, also. (Whelan 2000, p. 41)

Some members of the audience have been sitting at the table, and in this orientation to David's character, they have "become" his family. Other spectators have had to move toward the dining room and this table. They must jockey for position around this event. The dining room's proximity to the kitchen, in the next room, means the smell of coffee house food permeates this scene and the room is hot from the large ovens just beyond the door. The synesthetic effect of the scene is a curious paradox between the nurturing smells from the kitchen and the angry heat of the action.

It seems that we confront the spirit of the real in theatre, in education, and in any heartfelt relationship we have with others, when we experience our relationships—to each other, to our environment, to ourselves—in such a way that defies signification, or any way in which we might *speak* about the exact nature of these relationships. Site-specific theatre challenges the conventional forms of theatre and theatre education in that both to learn and practice such theatre, the student and practitioner must be open to the particular, sensual, and indeterminate qualities of an aesthetic engagement with the resource of creation: the site. However, those who create this way must also be open to the element that completes the trinity of creation: the witness. Therefore, it was essential for me to guide my students toward an understanding that their work must invite the public into the question of what they are creating, in such a way that the spectators feel implicated in some way, implicated in the event of their spectatorship. In that site-specific theatre is open to the indeterminacy of specific qualities of the site and its animation, there is a demand for the spectator to be open to this event, to be present as a witness. Tim Etchells says that "to witness an event is to be present at it in some fundamentally ethical way, to feel the weight of things and one's place in them, even if that place is simply, for the moment, as an on-looker" (1999, p. 18). As the dramaturgical strategies of *1800 Confessions Avenue* construct a theatrical-representational apparatus, and thereby signify an identity in relationship to 1800 College Avenue—the object of the performance—there is an awareness that this "object" is not a stable entity; that its plenitude in performance is fissured by a reliance on something which extends outside of itself, a "surplus" to representation. In *1800 Confessions Avenue,* the dramaturgical weave of the host and the ghost opens up the effects of this surplus, as a "substance" which resists the signification of identity, appropriation through history, technology, or other rational mastery.

This substance of the site resisting mastery can be equated with any object of desire. In theatre or education, it might be best likened to knowledge of one's subject or resource and of one's self. In September 2000, the first floor of 1800 College Avenue had remained relatively intact. Magellan's Global Coffee House existed mainly on this floor for its comfortable atmosphere. The second floor was where the washrooms were located, but otherwise it was mostly vacant, and scarred by failed renovation attempts. Perhaps the most common paranormal activity, reported by the staff of the coffee house, was the sound of a woman's voice singing at the top of the stairs. Sometimes, several times a week, the voice would be heard. Those new to the experience would rush to the top of the stairs, only to find silence and the gutted remains of the second floor. Perhaps the ghostly voice is the substance of Rose McKillop, and what we encounter when we try to find her has to do with our relationship to her memory. I think her haunting marks the object of desire of 1800 College Avenue because artists and audience alike would search in vain for Rose without fully realizing that she has no positive consistency, and our thoughts, images, enactments, and other representations of her are really just a positivization of a void—of a discontinuity opened in our present reality due to a ghost or the manifestation of a memory.

In the performance, Amber Fletcher musically adapted Robert Louis Stevenson's *Home No More to Me* and sang it at the top of the stairs, and on the line ". . . the kind hearts, the true hearts, that loved the place of old," in each performance I would always observe a spectator, as they had worked to get to the top of the stairs, looking as though they had attained something of themselves in what remained of this beloved "place of old."

The substance hunted like a ghost by my students and I, which exists in excess to 1800 College Avenue—as it becomes the object of desire, and curiosity, sadness, and ultimately, theatrical representation—engages the spectators in a process of "work" because it poses a question which aims at the heart of subjectivity, and by this I mean it aims at the heart of our spirit. At first glance, this may seem like a conventional philosophical problem. The witness-as-subject takes on the question posed by the performance, and as such enacts this critical force of negativity upon the positively given self or, in other words, embodies the question. However, here we have a notion of subjectivity that is the exact opposite. The subject is not a question, it is an answer, the "answer" of the real to the question by the symbolic order or, in this case, the theatrical representation of a house. It is not the subject asking the question. The subject-taken-as-spirit is the void of the impossibility of answering this question. The subject must work toward the answer of the question posed by the performance of this house because in a sense the question is unanswerable, yet the pursuit of the answer, the relationship created between the subject and the object of representation, which is the substance of this question, is the spiritual mystery of subjectivity itself.

In demanding that the witness be the subject of a question posed by the theatrical representation of a site, the dramaturgical strategies of site-specific theatre aim at the innermost, intimate kernel of subjectivity. As teaching, theatre, and the relationship of these practices touch reality, there may be an engagement with this place of the spirit at the very heart of subjectivity which cannot be symbolized, which is produced as a residue, a remnant, a leftover of every signifying operation; a hard core embodying *jouissance*, a problematic enjoyment, and as such an object that simultaneously attracts and repels us; it divides our desire and thus provokes us to work toward a response to how it haunts us. In my experience, the spiritual aspect of my own subjectivity exists only in so far as I experience it as some alien, positively given entity—the sounds of a woman being attacked beyond the walls of my room, the graffiti of the dead in a stairwell of a parliament building, the scars left on what was once a beautiful family home—and this experience, this *relationality* between the object of representation and the object within myself is my spirit, and it is the effect of site-specific theatre. In the face of this paradoxical effect, of the divided desire stimulated by the dramaturgy, there is the potential for the subject-as-witness to develop an ethical form of relating, an integrity toward the real, and toward the essence of its own spirit.

An Insight of Site versus Sight

Now, from a distance of a few years and several thousand kilometres, I am not sure if I believe in the ghost of Rose McKillop, but I certainly believe in the effects of my relationship with her, through the traces of her I found in her house. I will never forget the sensual qualities of my work in 1800 College Avenue: the light on the stairwell; the smells of the dust, the coffee, the wonderful food, and the house's decay, as a window would be opened after a rain storm; the sounds of our confessions alongside the confessional creaks and groans of the architecture's age; and simply, the feel of the place. When I walk into most classrooms, lecture halls, or theatres I wonder, why do we deny these sensual qualities of a live experience? Why is there such an emphasis on sitting behind bolted-down rows of chairs, sometimes with retractable desks, under florescent light, or alternatively in stalls and balconies, in the dark, just trying to get a better view? Just trying to see. When I think about this I am reminded of being in the dark myself, in a room in Regina, and that perhaps these other ways of experiencing the world are more traumatic and less controllable, but in this sense they are more real, which can be scary. However, we must face these "felt" qualities with our students, in our classes, in our theatre, as we must do in ourselves, in our dreams and our nightmares; we should learn to play with, and teach, what scares us most. In embracing the unknown perhaps we invite our first tentative encounters with spirit beyond classroom walls.

References

Etchells, T. (1999). *Certain fragments*. London: Routledge.

Freud, S. (1977). *The interpretation of dreams*. London: Harmondsworth.

McLucas, C. (1993). Brith Gof—Large scale site-specific theatre works: An illustrated lecture. Cardiff: Brith Gof.

Whalen, G. (2000). Our house: A report prepared for Theatre 250—The Host/The Ghost/The Witness—Collective dramaturgy assignment. University of Regina.

PART III

EMBODYING POETICS

Healing *Susto*

Fragments of Postcritical Pedagogy

I.

Leaving is never really leaving. In a sense, it is a false absence. The absence is similar to how light casts against an object. The object, unable to resist the persistence of the light, throws aside a distorted result. The blurry aftermath is persistent. It needs unattached attachment in order to exist. It dangles and weaves, elongates, shortens; it moves in syncopated rhythm in order to keep up with yet out of the way of its unpredictable host.

II.

I'm amazed that I didn't realize it sooner. Hindsight clarity amazes me dumb. You would have thought that the tight feeling in my stomach might have clued me in or that my writer's apprehension signaled something was wrong, something was missing. I thought maybe that I just hated writing. The anxiety I suffered every time I started a major writing assignment should somehow have let me know. Indeed, it would have, I suppose, had I not stopped paying attention, had I not disconnected, had I not run away.

III.

Sometimes when you talk about love, compassion, understanding, and connection people look at you as if you are a freak, a strange and dangerous thing. I have yet to muster the courage to talk openly about love in my classroom, but I strive for a loving perception. I have just now started to express publicly the necessity for compassionate understanding and connection. However, there is something about love that is still too dangerous for some, if not many. I have come to believe that the ideas and practices I find comforting, the things that allow for my tenuous safety, create danger for others.

IV.

Curranderismo: A hybrid healing tradition that incorporates the indigenous practices of the *Nahuatl* of Mexico and the spiritual Catholic traditions of Europe. These rituals are performed by one who is known as a *currandera* or *currandero* for the sole purpose of bringing one into spiritual, physical, mental, and emotional balance. The practice of *curranderismo* is controversial. Some consider *curranderas* and *curranderos* to be nothing more than quacks, illegitimate, sinister witch doctors whose sole purpose is to take one's money. It reflects a shadowed understanding of an ancient healing practice.

V.

Mother took us—my brothers and sisters and I—to the *curranderas* and *curranderos* when we were young. She warned us never to tell others about our spiritual adventures. She never explained why the silence was necessary. As I aged, I realized that this practice that provided tenuous comfort for me created judgment in others. "You believe in that stuff? Sounds like hocus pocus bull shit to me!" In a moment of weakness, I disclosed to a teenage peer about our trips to the *curranderas* and *curranderos*. That incident proved my mother right, I should never tell others about my spiritual adventures. Because I was young, because I was uncertain, and because I wanted to rebel against the authority of my mother, I fled—a mad flight from a spiritual world. Convincing myself that the "facts" were all that mattered and that detached Western logic would somehow save my soul from the shame of illegitimacy, from quackery, from all that is felt but unseen.

VI.

Susto: An *Nahuatl* understanding. Soul loss. A startled state of fright that injures one's spiritual aura; a fracturing shock that so overwhelms, pieces of the soul must scatter and run; their escape is thwarted, however, by the spiritual umbilical cords that tie them to the body; they hang damaged and diaphanous, both near and far. Feelings of absence ensue; the most effortful focus seems fuzzy, shadowy. Something is missing. Everything is distant and disconnected. Depression.

VII.

Mr. Morrison was my tenth-grade English teacher. He was a warm, sweet man with a sharp sense of humor. He would laugh one of those full-body laughs when something struck him as funny. I remember him sharing an anecdote in class—a sure sign that he trusted us. He told us the story of a student who received a graded essay from him. Mr. Morrison used to have micro dialogues in the margins of papers with his students. We would receive papers back with questions and comments such as "Really?" "How interesting." "I understand." "Have you ever considered . . . ," and, my favorite, "comma splice." This student, earnest in his attempt to learn from his teacher's feedback, could not at all figure out what Mr. Morrison meant by "frog meat." As the story goes, frog meat littered the bloody field that constituted the margins of this youth's essay. How strange. How mysterious. Odd. What ever could it mean? Frog meat. Peculiar. I now know that fragments can cause confusion.

VIII.

"You can do it, Denise. I really think you can." Mr. Morrison as cheerleader assured me that I really needed to be in an honors English class because, as he put it, I was a good writer. In addition, something inside told me to give it a try. So, I did because I believed Mr. Morrison wouldn't lead me astray.

Mr. Gentry, my eleventh grade English teacher, was not at all like Mr. Morrison. He was from the old school, the established school that didn't and doesn't like deviation from the norm, that believes hazing is tradition and tradition builds necessary character. Where critique is given as a means to explain how you fail but never to explain how you succeed, a harsh pedagogy born of "facts" and detachment. It is a tradition of established legitimacy, a logic that enables only the survival of the fittest. I was beginning to feel like frog meat, fragmented and cold, bloody. I ended up in summer school that year and earned an "A" to replace the unacceptable "D" that I received in Mr. Gentry's Honors English class. However, despite getting it "right" the second time, something was missing.

IX.

Currandera and Currandero: the healing practitioners of *curranderismo*. Women and men who have learned the rituals and traditions that bring the mind, body, and spirit back into balance. When the *currandera* heals *susto,* she engages in a variety of rituals. Usually, the *currandera* begins any healing relationship with *platicas*, dialogues, with the afflicted to get a sense of the trauma and to determine the extent of how severe the fright is. Once she understands the situation, she then plans a series of rituals and prayers that will help guide the fractured spirit back into the body so that the afflicted can strengthen and heal. In one instance, one might need herbal sweeping to cleanse the aura of heavy emotions that have settled on the spirit, weighing it down. In another, one might need a *bano*, a water bath drawn with herbal tinctures and oils to seal the goodness of these preparations onto the body, fortifying a weakened demeanor. In another, one might need to journal through the experience, drawing the trauma up, transferring it onto the page and then willfully and symbolically loosening and releasing the emotional grip that restricts the spirit. Once the preparatory rituals and prayers have been completed and the afflicted one has done the necessary preparation, the *currandera* can then begin the slow and gentle process of calling back the soul fragments to rejoin into a whole. The detached fragments, depending on how long they have suffered, will have to re-acquaint themselves with the rest of the soul, a process that cannot be rushed.

My soul was fractured and fragmented. There were several small blows that settled over time, creating a need to fly from the hardened world of institutionalized education, and yet, I couldn't leave school. Many of those blows resulted from an internalized understanding of what others concluded about who I was supposed to be as a student. I have been nothing but a nontraditional student. I was never ever quick. I was never ever an over achiever. I was never ever interested in competing against my more or less capable peers. However, I loved learning. I loved engaging ideas that invited me to wrap my struggling mind around them, to massage them into healthful understanding, toning atrophied muscles. I, like a soul fractured by *susto*, dangled damaged and diaphanously, fearful of letting go. What would happen if I released my grip?

I didn't visit the *currandera* to help call my soul back from the fright of institutionalized learning primarily because I didn't know that I was ailing. It wasn't until that one encounter, that so very important *platica*, talk, with my English professor who encouraged me to continue writing because I was so good at it. I had no idea. In that moment, all of it started to make sense—the anxiety, the self-defeat, the fear and the frustration. I had no idea that my writing apprehension was born from the fracturing words of just a few but significant encounters with others who were steeped in "us versus them" logics and practices, teacher vs. student, right vs. wrong. Now, as a pedagogue, what would I do? Whose words and actions would I allow to infuse my own praxis? What method and methodology would I develop to suggest to colleagues and students my postcritical stance, my commitment to healing fragmenting wounds?

X.

Gloría Anzaldúa (1999) writes:

> It is not enough to stand on the opposite river bank, shouting questions, challenging patriarchal, white conventions. A counterstance locks one into a duel of oppressor and oppressed; locked in mortal combat, like the cop and the criminal, both are reduced to a common denominator of violence. . . . Because the counterstance stems from a problem with authority—outer as well as

inner—it's a step towards liberation from cultural domination. But it is not a way of life. At some point, on our way to a new consciousness, we will have to leave the opposite bank, the split between the two mortal combatants somehow healed so that we are on both shores at once and, at once, see through serpent and eagle eyes. (pp. 100–101)

Anzaldúa's call for healing, for the ability to foster an empathic attitude that allows one to see as both the serpent and the eagle, as damaged and dangling, as caller and healer comes closest to my understanding of what a postcritical pedagogy necessitates. The challenge lies in subduing the fear that drives "us versus them" so that "us and them" thoughts and practices finally find solace and rectitude through a willful knowing that generates active compassion and a softened, loving perception. However, empathy, compassion, softness, and love should not be construed as weakness, passivity, or indifference. To do so only reifies the belief that aggressive attitudes and actions are superior to and more meaningful than quieter ones, and, ultimately, misses the point. Instead, I want to consider strength in stillness as a means for healing the split between the "two mortal combatants." I want to engage the paradox and strive to see as both "us and them," damaged and healer, student and teacher.

Latina feminist Maria Lugones (1990) resists feminist scholar Marilyn Frye's notion that love is the bedrock of "unconditional servitude." Lugones knows love as the means to identify with others, to have connection with them. She recognizes, however, that many are taught to perceive difference with arrogance, an attitude that in turn promotes resistance to identification with others, and one that ultimately brings about the unwillingness to love. This unwillingness, this arrogance, must be released in order for the love of other to germinate. However, I know that even the most willing defensively resist loving others (I know I sometimes do); the thought of embracing a stranger (a student) with warmth and compassion is too frightening, a chance too risky to take.

Yoga master Erich Schiffman (1996) claims that yogic practice fosters a "release from fear [that] finally promotes a full flowing of love" and "a softened perception of the world." Schiffman suggests that when one has let go of everything he or she does not need—arrogance, for example, or the attitude of Anzaldúa's "mortal combatants"—all that is left is love. It is in this state of love, this softened perception, that one discovers that there is no need for defensiveness; one can finally choose to "remain undefended" when facing a critical and emotionally violent world. The choice to remain undefended is not an act of passive indifference. It is not a means for ignoring injustice or oppression in the world. Instead, it allows the possibility for fostering an alternative attitude that promotes the gentleness necessary to diffuse the contentiousness of "us vs. them." It allows the notion of "authoritative center" to become contested, as well as reclaimed as one becomes "centered," creating a paradox that requires a release from fear that eventually promotes the connection suggested by Lugones and the loving and softened perception claimed by Schiffman.

Neither Lugones nor Schiffman uses the term "vulnerable" when describing these ideas, but it is quite clear that they are calling for an unguarded and exposed sensibility. However, to move into a space of vulnerability in a postcritical sense means that one must be centered enough to move into that unguarded position.

Dennis Mumby (1997) writes that "the phrase *discourse of vulnerability* is intended to evoke the ways in which the postmodern intellectual has given up the 'authority game' as a uniquely positioned arbiter of knowledge claims" (p. 14). The knowing subject as central to his or her world where theorizing is based on only his or her lived experience is displaced because postmodernism acknowledges multiple truths, multiple experiences, multiple stories. As a result, one is vulnerable to the multiplicity of assertions based on the lived experiences of various others that come into play in communicative praxis. The notion of a definitive center gets complicated given that contexts are always in flux, centers are always moving.

Erich Schiffman's yogic philosophy (Schiffman as *currandero*) compels me to live in the paradox of vulnerability. He writes:

> We are ignorant of our true nature, our real identity. We don't know who we really are. This is because we have never experienced ourselves directly. We have never stayed "home" long enough to experience the truth about ourselves. We are not encouraged to do this. Instead we accepted as true what other people told us about ourselves. And, unfortunately, we were taught by people who, in all likelihood, and through no fault of their own, did not actually know. (p. 5)

Schiffman suggests that we actively seek ourselves by systematically letting go "of all [our] learned preconceptions about [ourselves] and then stay . . . present and open minded for the experience" (8). Any fear associated with these preconceptions are then cleared, allowing for a "full flowing of love" to take place. With Schiffman's urging, Mr. Gentry's assertions about my performance as an eleventh-grade high school honors English student gently fall away and the scattered fragments begin to gather back into a more loving whole. I now have the emotional room to begin the healing work so that I see Mr. Gentry no longer as a mortal combatant, but as someone who believed his (centered) way of doing things was the only way of doing things. I am able to see his limitations, even though he was most likely never able to see mine in a way that mattered beyond the content of eleventh-grade honors English.

XI.

A few years have passed since my last visit to the *currandera*. I wonder why I have not been back during that time. What blocks my return? I think about my current position as an assistant professor in a mid-sized state university on the eastern-most edge of the Midwest. I think about how its demands have pressed upon me in such a way that my need for the spiritual, for the *currandera*, has been compromised. "I don't have time," I anxiously tell myself, doing everything I must in order to perform "good professor." I know I need to wind down, to slow to center, so that I can gather the fragments caused by the craziness of being too busy. In the moments of insane multitasking, the centeredness of yoga gently calls to me, reminding me of its soothing breath and metaphoric pose. A voice inside asks me to release the arrogance I've developed toward self; it lovingly wants me to let it go so that love can fill its place. The *currandera* calls, too. She reminds me of the growth possible if I, ironically, let go. She beckons while I write these words, when I stir sugar into my coffee, or as I plan my next lesson. She reminds me of the work I have yet to do, of the calling back I must be willing to proclaim. I have to become my own *currandera*, she whispers, I have to learn to be my own healing practitioner.

References

Anzaldúa, G. (1999). *Borderlands/la frontera: The new mestiza*. San Francisco: Aunt Lute Books.

Frye, M. (1983).*The politics of reality: essays in feminist theory*. Trumansburg, NY: Crossing Press.

Lugones, M. (1990). Playfulness, world-traveling, and loving perception. In G. Anzaldúa (Ed.), *Making face, making soul: Haciendo caras* (pp. 390–402). San Francisco: Aunt Lute Books.

Mumby, D. (1997). Modernism, postmodernism, and communication studies: A re-reading of an ongoing debate. *Communication Theory, 7*(1), 1–28.

Schiffman, E. (1996). *Yoga: the spirit and practice of moving into stillness*. New York: Pocket Books.

Leaning Absolutes

Honoring the Detours in Our Lives

Moss and lichen drenched the trees leaning over the Burrard Inlet as my black lab and I did our daily walk. It was a lavender gray winter day, and light rain fell on my shoulders as I brought my still-recovering body around the inlet. I was captivated during the whole walk by the thought that the Creator who formed these hundreds of arched trees had been perceived for so many centuries as a God of absolutes. I tried to find even one lone tree standing perfectly straight. It was not to be found. Straight trees did not exist in this landscape. All were bent, crooked, ultimately leaning their torsos toward each other, toward the salt water's edge, and toward myself. They seemed to be in an ever-present conversation, their branches waving in the gentle wind; alive, vibrant, and bowed. I briskly walked, breathing in my own paradox of not being able to live in the absolutes set before me, the continual choices of either/or, both large and small.

Creation leaned too much on the erotic side to be able to think of a straight God. What a concept, a straight God, or a straight curriculum for that matter, or is there a crooked God or is it about having a sensuous God? Is it about a Creator that delights in the sensuality of creation, moss, lichen, and mud—a God of mud. Yes, we were made out of the earth, the mud earth, dust-to-dust, clay-to-clay, tree-to-tree, and leaning-to-leaning. We walk the earth as well, straight up and down, but dare I say we ever really walk perfectly straight?

Leaning into creation, letting creation lean into me. The ongoing dialogue of bodies leaning: body of tree, body of flesh. The trees' leaves have shed, and their naked trunks and branches stretch in glory. They all stretch, none holding back, all leaning in communion, an order all of their own. How could anyone think that we as mere humans could impose an order on the eros of creation? Respecting its own internal order, its own rhythm, it has much to teach us about being and living. Of course tribal peoples established these connections from the beginning of time. Do those trees resist the way they lean, or do they just lean proudly, elegantly? Absolutely leaning. My dancer body craves leaning, stretching, bending, reaching, in the open space. It never thrived in classical ballet, although it was all good foundation to relate to gravity, and to ultimately know how to lean. My body needs flamenco now.

The path, the journey, whatever metaphor one uses for the roads we take in life, is filled with curves, detours, branches of eros leaning out to us in all directions. As much as we plan the curriculum of life, the book, the lesson plan, the marriage, the family or career, they all have lives of their own. In fact, one thing is for sure, the plan will mess up, and we may even be invited into a spirituality of messiness. There is a whole other path we follow apart from the external realities in our lives. It is a path of soul, but a path of body, too. In essence, paying attention to soul is paying attention to body. Paying attention to body is paying attention to soul.

The tradition of Buddhism has a cherished word, "meitri," which ultimately means to have compassion for everything that comes in our lives. Rumi (1995) tells us to welcome everything, even the uninvited guests, in his poem, "The Guest House": "Be grateful for whoever comes . . . as a guide from beyond" (p. 109).

In the same vein Jesus said, several centuries before, to entertain strangers, for they may be angels. Angels, strangers, and uninvited guests come in many forms. Could eros be an uninvited guest? Do we push it aside so we only see it articulated in the objectification of flesh and perhaps miss the life-giving movements of our own hearts and gestures, the feel of a leaning tree, or in a child squirming at a desk?

How can we lean into the uninvited guests of our lives whether that is people, experiences, illnesses, broken plans, or both the delight and limitations of our own bodies? It takes strength to lean. Endurance. I come to leaning into my own changed dreams. The earthquake of the soul has brought shifts; what propelled and fueled me at one time in my life does not now. Before teaching in a Faculty of Education I taught for many years in theological graduate schools, and in fact was one of the few women teaching. I had my heart set on integrating the artistic and bodily ways of knowing into spirituality in this context. However, as the years passed I increasingly did not fit into the boxes of the institutions I was involved in, and in fact the last place I ever thought I would find myself is in a secular institution working with teachers. I can now say that I have more freedom to live from the center of who I am and teach, research, and write in ways that honor me as an artistic, bodily, scholarly, and feminine human being. I presently work with more students exploring ideas of spirituality than I probably would have in the more rigid boundaries of a theological context. I went on a detour and found home. This does not convey the many hours and years of turmoil, leaving a world I had grown to love, even in the midst of its difficulties and limitations.

I can only lean from my old dreams so I can recover or uncover new ones. I wait. It has been partially revealed, but not totally. I perhaps have not leaned long enough. I planned the course, yet the course planned me; a detour, a curve, an invitation to watch the green moss caress the tree, to delight in bringing the body to the practice of teaching, ultimately the practice of engaging life. What do the recurring detours have to teach me? I ponder how many times I have tried to push myself into environments that really did not suit me in the first place. Mechthild of Madgeburg tells us from medieval times that a fish cannot drown in its own water. How long does it take to find our own water? Leaning into life, we may find it. I keep hoping the path may be straighter or smoother, actually less messy. Somehow this does not happen and I wonder why I am still surprised by the detours and curves along the path. However, it is only a matter of time when suffering teaches us to let go, release the very absolutes that are grasping at the freedom of our body-souls.

I ask myself how I honor the detours in my life. The unexpected curve, the surprise angle, the disappointing turn. Are the detours actually the path to the life that really wants to live in me? In us? Are the detours the way of migrating to the heart of my own life? I never see detours this way in the beginning. Only from afar do I see their wisdom, do I see their intrinsic beauty, the beauty that almost begins with terror as Rilke so provocatively says. Detours are like the wind. One never knows when they will come, arise out of the destined path. They come unannounced. Even if there are signs along the road, we never truly know what to expect. Otherwise they would not be a detour. I can think of all the times there has been a detour while I have been driving, and I had no idea which neighborhood I would be taken into, or how I would get out of there for that matter. Detours sing with curvilinear sounds and diagonal gestures. They are often necessary, but I'd rather avoid them. Detours in my life are even more of a bother. I have been so schooled in persisting in a linear fashion that even a spiral interruption is troubling at times. Even though I would consider myself a spiral thinker, a spiral dancer. I live and dwell in the spirals. Nothing is usually straight. However, I still have some preconception that the road will be smooth. A direct path. Even so, I hate direct paths. I like nooks and crannies, unforeseen rocks and stones, foliage spilling out and interrupting the soil.

There is a time to have deep compassion on all our detours.

Detours are what artists do when they create.

They often happen in the middlings of things.

It is where imagination erupts.

It is where life erupts

and we are born

anew.

I keep returning to the wisdom that there are a thousand ways to frame a life. And yet perhaps it is about living a frameless life. How do we get to the life that truly wants to live in us? We sometimes need to cross passes, a mountain pass of the soul, leave that which has even been carved out as precious: jobs, relationships, countries. These leavings are sometimes by choice, and other times by life's circumstances. They are happenstances, the paints on the canvas of our lives. In my own life, it is loss and grief that has been a recurring theme of a detour. It is the loss of how "I thought life should be." I have come to see that what I need to lose most is my prescribed way of looking at how I think life should turn out. What causes pain, over and over again, is the way I frame my own story, the way I frame the curriculum of my life.

Life means continuous education. We are schooled in the soul of life, a form of education that is not much different from the classroom. Where life is a classroom of formation for growth, the classroom is a formation for life—if we let it. However, it may not always turn out as we expect. I tell my student teachers that no matter how good their education, how amazing their mentors, and how well thought out their curriculum plans may be, ultimately they need to rely on their resources within them to be effective teachers. Teaching is a bodily act, and we must engage every part of the knowledge available to us: kinesthetic, cognitive, intuitive, artistic, perceptual; the list goes on and on. No one can predict the course of life's events, universally or personally, which will affect the learning experience. I am invited into leaning into different ways of understanding my own life and the elements that comprise it—my teaching, writing, and parenting. I need to reframe the way I see, the way I hear, the way I understand my life.

Frames and Fragments

Frames
Borders
boundaries of clay
impression marks
of flesh

There is life
and there is
the way we see life
They are not
the same.

I have frames
for the way I see my life
Stories of interpretation
layers of hermeneutic
madness and discovery
of how it is
how it should be
how it was

What does it take to
reframe the way I see
the way I be
the way I live
the way I teach, write, dance, love,

Pain is our greatest teacher
My old way of seeing
the narrative of "myself"
has exhausted its term.
I am not served by it.

Perhaps I should take my own "story"
and rewrite it,
paint it with different colors
ochre instead of red
prose instead of poetry
hope instead of despair
spaciousness instead of closure

How can we look at each other with "new eyes"
l u m i n o u s compassion
unless we look at ourselves with different lens,
light of early morning
where all is magical -
first born
tenderly wild
I want to step through my own frames
my own interpretation of stories
fall into deep listening
unclench into heart space
soften the gaze onto myself
l i v e
frameless
borderless
with frames of love
borders of love
towards myself
and others

a place of no judgement
of endings/beginnings/middlings
stop picking at the back of the tapestry
noticing only cut threads and knots
but relish in the new colors forming

new designs shaping
fresh textures emerging
see the beauty of back and front

Cherishing the fragments
little stories go into
the bigger story
the one we all weave together
of absolute complexity and paradox
of dwelling as earthlings
among garlic and amethysts
dirt and diamonds
weeds and wisteria.

Perhaps all we do is
bear fragments
of love and life
partial and full
beginnings and endings

Even a fragment of old woven cloth
can be stunning
if it is framed beautifully
with lots of space and clear glass

I want to view my life
with new eyes
the tattered fragments
with precious hues
this may be really
what the beginning is.

I wrote this poem in a time when I really needed to find compassion on my own life. After a twenty-year marriage dissolving, and the years of grief for the layers of loss that shake and shape the soul, I needed new ways of seeing. However this is not a one-time act, a one-time poem. I usually dance this poem, sometimes with someone only reading the words, and at other times with someone reading it and accompanying me with an instrument. I also include an artist's frame and literally dance through the frame, break the frame, and eventually loosen its hold on my life. The visceral act of dancing the words is an ongoing invitation for the words to become flesh. I am remade in the words, for my own trap is to continue to go back into the old stories, which hold me from finding more inner spaciousness in my life. I have danced this for a variety of audiences, including teachers and preservice teachers, a concert setting, and even in the middle of a sermon in a church. It is a timeless truth, and as a practice I need to find ways to physically and spiritually honor the detours in my own life. We all do. We need to tend our lives with tenderness. Tending the stories with new stories, new frames, ultimately new eyes.

I have been pondering the relentlessness of gentleness these days. How reshaping our ways of seeing is truly an act of gentleness, a way of tending the earth, and the flesh of our spirits. I have learned that it is often much easier to find acts of random kindness, acts of gentleness, toward others than myself. Those of us who are in the academy can be particularly hard schoolmasters on ourselves. Responsibility is not one of our problems, if anything we are too responsible. We have forgotten the art of play and pause, passion and paucity. It is true, even in realms of education and spirituality we are better "human doings" than "human beings." One of the aspects of my own character that propels me from "doing" to "being" is impatience. Even though some might say, "I'm a patient person," I have come to see that this is really only looking from the outside. It is as if it is almost always easier to be a good parent in public. One only needs to ask one of my three boys to see how patient I really am. Coupled with the fact that impetuousness lies at the heart of my soul, I am not given to getting an award in the area of patience. This aspect works great when I am performing or teaching improvisation, but not always in cultivating and tending tenderness in my own life. It may still be decades that I keep learning in the school of patience.

Many of my lessons in life come from my intimate connection with nature. Creation is a lover to me, and I partake of this visual and sensory feast daily through walking. Walking has become my spiritual practice; my litany where I rediscover the textures of the earth's soul. I walk the path daily around the Burrard Inlet in Port Moody, British Columbia, and it is here where I enter the earth as libation. I slow my mind down and loosen my grasp from the one hundred thousand details of balancing motherhood and university teaching. I walk the curvilinear path to disrobe the details of "doing" and enter "being." Walking the inlet's curve I smell the earth as lover, I drink in the scent of green, and I am summoned to human beingness.

I have walked the Inlet's curves and sinews for almost a decade. I know where the path rises and falls, is moist and dry, where there are secret spots for looking at wild birds. I sometimes walk it as a woman with a mission, a vigorous stride toward the torso of earth. At other times I walk it as a foreigner, a visitor on the moss, longing for a spot of comfort and meander off the trail. On other days, I allow my mind to get out of what has been called "monkey mind" and settle down to the place where I begin to hear the soft voice of spirit, the place to hear my own voice, the voice of vision and heart, the voice imbued with intuitive tenderness. Walking is my prayer, the place of deep listening. Simone Weil (1952) has said, "absolutely unmixed attention is prayer" (p. 106). In walking I attend. I attend to the nuances of the creation in the external world, and I attend to the nuances in my internal world. I used to try to choose between meditating and walking, and now I see that my walking is my meditation. It is in moving that I find stillness. Not a frozen stillness, but a stillness that is deeply alive. A stillness where soul resides. A stillness where essence is smelled. It is a water walk, an edge I saunter on which hugs water life, waterfowl, the sea's jewels.

One of the jewels to me since last summer is my recurring encounter with a blue heron. This blue heron stands and waits with fierce elegance. It is vigilant in being in what I would call a moving stillness. I am learning patience from the blue heron. The capacity to have "patience with presence" as my friend Wilbur said in a conversation the other day. I am schooled at the edge of the sea in what I need to know.

Crane Light

Crane me with your light
breathe elegant openings
of gray green
teach me simplicity
waiting blue heron

I watch you
minor shifts in moving
I've already squiggled
a dozen times
while you peer tall
on barnacled stage

I never saw
stillness so refined
sea ballerina
extension time
I unravel moments
of worry
you are pure being

The heron has become my teacher.
I could sit every day in heron's presence.
Regain feminine strength to wait.
Wait for the wind that turns the head.
Soften the glance unto oneself.
Remember the heron's dance
an adagio of quiet.

What would it be like to welcome all of life with extended arms, open palms, expansive chest, wide eyes, relaxed heart? What if, just what if, the detours of our lives were the way of the universe to direct us to our own true path? How would we then look on our shortcomings, failures, or limitations? How does all of that work into evaluative methods or how we look at our colleagues or our students? It certainly does not work into the tenure process or report cards.

I am coming to see that it does not just take an honoring of new ways of seeing our own stories, really an honoring of a spirituality of messiness, but a compassionate patience with all that happens in our lives, even the places of discord and paradox. Moreover, it does not mean that we may be smiling, because I know I am a feisty gal and there is no way anything comes easy to me. However, I can be invited into the school of tenderness, the school of gentleness, but not a gentleness that is meek, but one of strength and elegance.

Ultimately this process takes a theology of suffering, something we are not so good at in the throes of a culture of immediacy, so typical of western culture. I am drawn to cultures who hold suffering and even grief as an avenue for spiritual formation. Our capacity for joy and suffering all come from the same font. It is our capacity to engage richly in this world with all its splendor and horror, to feel what we need to feel. It is not an easy path. It is messy. In order to create anything of beauty an artist needs to get messy. The painter will get paint on the shirt; the dancer will get injuries to the body; the musician may also have a physical injury. It takes hours of just messing around with the stuff of art in order to create beauty, even if that beauty is dissonant. This is why kids are so good at doing art. They are not yet afraid of getting messy. They think this is part of the glory of the process—and it is—until adults tell them otherwise.

So I am proposing that we think about a spirituality of messiness: to let our classrooms get messy enough to delve into life, delve into paint, delve into the body; to let our friendships get messy enough to let conflict reside; to live with incongruence; to let our hearts be open enough to hold the inconsistencies that many spiritual practices and religions offer; to bring the tend back into tenderness; to truly nurture what is calling out to us; to migrate to our own life. Follow the detour and thus follow the heart. It just may happen through the detour of the body. After all, the soul and body really need each other.

I have been invited to lean into new frames, new questions, and ultimately new answers. In this place, there is more spaciousness for paradox, and it is here where I return again and again: Paradoxicalness; in praise of paradox; in the heart of a spirituality of messiness is paradox. Mystery keeps beckoning me to its shoulder. I leave in wonder for the leaning absolutes.

References

Rumi. (1995). *The essential Rumi.* (C. Barks, Trans.). San Francisco: HarperCollins.
Weil, S. (1952). *Gravity and grace.* (E. Craufurd, Trans.). London: Routledge & Kegan Paul.

The Heart's Geography

Compassion as Practice

Commitments of the spirit have engaged me for many years. I began regular practice of meditation thirty years ago, studying with an eastern meditation teacher in the tantric tradition of Kashmir Shaivism. Within a few years, I began my own teaching of meditation, which continues today and remains a foundation of my pedagogical and personal practice. While I felt strong resonances with the texts of Kashmir Shaivism and its mystical doctrines of the heart, there were points of tension. I noted that sadly far more male voices spoke in these texts than women's, and while a significant personal mentor in my own life had been an eastern male, my journey would be shaped and guided by the needs of a woman living and working in the institutional world of the west. As a woman, I felt informed and inspired by eros, by desire and longing, by the passions of the feeling body. I wondered how, as a living presence, I could offer my understandings freed from the limiting contexts of dogma or religious authority. Eventually, it was in the depths of personal somatic experience and in the images and stories of daily life that I crafted a phenomenology of the heart. I invite the reader to engage with me here in exploring the regions and meanings of the heart as the central space in a pedagogy of feeling.

In the tantric tradition the state of spiritual liberation is described as *hrydayangamibhuta*, a Sanskrit term commonly translated by the phrase "become something that moves in the heart" (Muller-Ortega, 1989, p. 2).

This conception/experience of the heart that moves is a unity of both se-
mantic and somatic meaning. The heart moves and is moved, and the experience of this awakened heart sustains and inspires my pedagogical practice. My perspective is phenomenological—giving attention to the heart as
it is immediately experienced in the self and with others. In exploring this
region of the awakened heart, I resist traditional cultural/religious concep-
tualizations of the heart, preferring to engage the metaphoric materiality of
images, stories, and experiences—a poetics of the living heart. I wonder
how the heart is restricted, restrained, immobilized, and conversely, what
conditions, practices, and attitudes might awaken movement and expansion. Paul Muller-Ortega (1989) in his exploration of the tantric tradition of
Kashmir Shaivism notes that "notions of contraction and expansion of the
Heart are directly related to the spiritual conditions of ignorance or enlightenment of the individual soul" (p. 122).

In tantric phenomenology, the heart is described as both method and at-
tainment, practice (upaya), and fulfillment. Through practices of the heart
we move toward awakening and expanding consciousness. A heartfelt
practice requires attentiveness to the stillness and movement of experience—to the multiple tightenings, contractions, fluidities, and expansions
of immediate somatic experience. Attentiveness is the doorway to a new
curriculum of breath, silence, and listening—listening in the body, listening to feeling, listening to the ordinary experiences of life—hearing (and
seeing) with the heart. It is in the ordinary, disregarded or forgotten phe-
nomena of the everyday that we discover insight and freedom. From the ordinary we distill the essence of human/heart experience.

Fundamental to this inquiry into the heart is the premise that the body is
a site of knowledge; therefore, lived experience in the body is central. This
concept represents a departure from perspectives governed by the duality of
thought and spirit—in which enlightenment involves a movement away
from the body to some higher, distant, transcendent sphere of being. The
moveable heart that I describe is an embodied heart offering an awareness of
the immanence of the infinite in the quotidian—one that invites and dis-
solves contradictions of flesh and spirit into a unity of presence. I speak of
embodiment as a listening in the body, a presence of body in the pedagogy of
practice. In earlier phenomenological reflections (Denton, 1998), I described
the heart as sited in the center of the chest—in the bodily space known in
yogic traditions as the heart *chakra*. This is not the physical heart, but
rather a visceral, pulsing territory of sensation and consciousness. In this

chapter, I address how we might be lifted away from our common perceptions of the heart, from a constraining set of definitions and images. I ask how we can ground ourselves, and our practice as educators in the insights, wisdom, peace, and compassion of the awakened heart.

Gestures of the Heart: Toward a Pedagogical Practice

When the Heart is in a state of contraction the awakened awareness of the individual self is in fact a state of ignorance. But when this contraction ceases to function, then the true nature of the Self shines forth. (Abhinavagupta qtd. in Muller-Ortega, 1989, p. 122)

Narratives of Contraction

When I am dry—where is the rasa—the juice of life? I speak mechanically—in appropriate phrases. I smile pleasantly—a smile solidified by years of practice. Many students recognize my face. Can I remember their names? A young woman speaks to me in my office. She closes the door as she begins to describe her experience of date rape and how this is affecting her in-class performance. I listen with calibrated compassion. But where is the heart in all of this? Where is the feeling? What am I feeling? What is she feeling? How am I to respond?

As educators integrating spirituality in our classroom practice how can we invite the true nature of the Self to shine forth? It seems a lofty challenge. In the midst of experiences that are never predictable and often troubling, how do we offer inspiration and light? My own practice has often been informed by the unpredictable—those surprise attacks and sudden irruptions that confront and inspire new directions of thought, action, and feeling. My longing to experience an expansion of consciousness was fuelled by an early and painful experience with my meditation teacher.

I approach my teacher, a swami from India, and ask him for a name—a common practice in a circle of disciples. He assigns Sanskrit names that are believed to reflect the deepest nature of those who ask. A translator repeats my request. My teacher responds with a thundering gaze. His voice resonates in me for days. In translation the words that remain are "Why haven't you expanded?" I feel unnamed. My heart and body tighten in the grip of guilt. It is only years later that I come to recognize the name—the challenge of the name—Why haven't I expanded?

In my experience of naming it was the "grip of guilt" that contracted the heart. As I judged myself, I tightened viscerally and emotionally. Despite all my disciplined efforts (meditation, chanting, and so forth), I was still not "good enough." The expansive self, the idealized, liberated, enlightened, transcendent self still eluded me. Feelings of self-doubt and disgust were memorialized and inscribed in my flesh. These sensations marked a return to the body, and although unknown to me at the time, a return to the heart. In the tightened, hardened heart, I made an early visceral connection that later illumined my understanding and pedagogical practice.

My continuing exploration of this question has found its way into my teaching. In classroom contexts, when I engage students in meditative exercises, we breathe into the heart center, into the heart chakra, attending to images, sensations, and feelings within. Students routinely report experiences of the heart as "hard," "tight," "frozen," "stony"—images of tightening and contraction. I wonder what impressions are stored here that their reportage is so uniform. Developing an awareness of this feeling of contraction is often a student's first step toward an expansion of consciousness. I attempt to evoke this awareness in an experiential exercise. I ask students to think of something they fear or detest. I offer my own irrational but visceral aversion to blood tests. We move into a meditative/imaginative practice where students visualize the distasteful object. I encourage them to move closer to it—to try to touch it. Physical and emotional responses to this experience include disgust, anxiety, physical tensing, distancing, and nausea. Students are then invited to imagine something or someone loved. "See if you can touch this," I say. Reactions described here are feelings of warmth, softness, connection, and compassion. I liken this experience to the immediate experiencing of self. When judgment clouds this inner relationship we distance or objectify the self. In this sense the visceral/emotional experience of contraction/judgment is what divides the self and contracts or limits consciousness. As we gather impressions of judgment the heart contracts and solidifies. Participants in meditation workshops across the years give voice to these contractions,

> A woman speaks of an icy stoniness around her heart. Her friend describes a thorny prickliness. Earlier a man has imagined an iceberg in his chest, and another woman sees a tight, thick rope encircling her heart. My own images are of stone—the stone heart. Together we experience an awareness

of physical density. My friend, a movement therapist, writes to me, "You speak of holding experience—that it is a tightness that becomes stone—yet earth is about holding—holds physical matter together as matter." Why haven't I expanded?

In ancient tantric texts, one reads of the malas—psychological limitations that restrict the free movement of consciousness. Karma mala is the limiting condition of "doing good or evil" (Singh, 1990, pp. 64–65)—the tendency to judge experience. When I judge my experience, I contract. Judging my feeling, I note a constriction in the heart. I notice that the heart's density (tightness) increases. I want to move from myself, from what has been seen. I notice this also when others judge me, when criticism launched is harsh or brutal—an attack against the self—"You are so stupid." In descriptions of anava mala, one reads that it brings about the sense of extreme smallness in the self because of "considering itself imperfect" (Singh, 1990, p. 64). When I am contracted I feel small. I feel limited. I seem to shrink in stature. These are not only metaphors but transcripts of somatic response.

In the meanings of mayiya mala, one finds the "apprehension of all objects as different" (Singh, 1990, p. 64). I notice how the tightening body, the defensive body, separates from experience. The world becomes a tight place. In this defensive state I launch my own attacks—visceral and verbal tightenings of gesture and speech. The gesturing voice is hollow or harsh.

I wonder, how do we can keep these malas—these limiting tendencies of consciousness—out of the classroom? For they are there. Built deeply into the institutional fabric of evaluation, regimentation, and command. Is there a mala-free zone? Can we create one? How do we shift from images of contraction to awaken the movement of the heart? In a step towards understanding, I use a simple object to conjure an image—a large black pillow. Presenting the pillow as the self, I begin to clutch together pieces of its material—the gathering of impressions—the material of a life—"I am not good enough," "I am not loved," and so forth. With each new impression, the pillow tightens and contracts. Later, under the caress of a gentle hand, the folds of material soften and relax into their original form (Denton, 1998).

Others imagine a small flame in the heart that seems to melt the icy regions of the self. Relaxing into the stone, into the flame, contractions in the heart ease and soften. Often in meditation exercises, students spontaneously touch their hearts. A gentle caress seems to soothe the tightenings of tissue. Visceral images of pillow, stone, and flame offer opportunities to engage the embodied structures of consciousness—to transform these structures.

Feeling as Mantra

Embracing feeling is risky territory. However, as Georg Feuerstein (1990) notes "self contraction is first and foremost a contraction of feeling" (p. 196). If we are to open spaces for the self, we must risk the wilderness of feeling. It is feeling that hardens and tightens in the heart. When our feelings are hurt, we erect defenses; we distance; we protect; we shut down. Feeling offers a return to the heart—feeling as movement, responsiveness, sensation, and emotion. As we recognize the sources of our own contraction images and stories, meditative and performative practices can inspire an awakening, a stirring, an enlivening and expansion of the heart through feeling.

What does it mean to invite feeling into our classrooms? How do we navigate this territory? What do we risk? As we stir the heart with feeling we dance on the edge of the unknown—the margins of desire, eros, pleasure, and pain. In my classes these phrases recur: "follow your feeling," "listen to your feeling." In Shaivism this movement of the heart is referred to as spanda—the vibration, flutter or throb of the Infinite in the heart (Muller-Ortega, 1989, p. 118). Learning to attend to this sensation/vibration is a first step. Through an absorption in feeling, consciousness begins to settle in the heart—pulling awareness viscerally into the present body. The gift of feeling is that "in all these intense emotional states . . . all other mental activities cease of themselves" (Singh, 1990, p. 104). Feeling acts as a mantra that calls consciousness home. From this perspective all experience—both agonies and ecstasies—may act as a point of entry to the heart. Râmakantha, a tenth-century mystic, offers a warning here. "These emotional states serve, to the awakened one, as a means for realizing the abiding Spanda if they throw him into a reflective recollection of his essential I-consciousness, not if they involve him in their own experience" (Râmakantha qtd. in Singh, 1980, p. 104). The caution offered here is simple—follow the feeling into the heart, into the self's embodied response, but don't lose yourself in the feeling. The emotion is a vehicle.

In class today a woman shares that she has difficulty understanding the read-ings. She cannot find a point of entry. A psychology student finds the readings easier to enter. The language is familiar. Some texts are easier to enter. Some experiences are easier to enter. They are familiar, known. Meaning can be easily apprehended through rational thought. There are pathways that indi-cate the point of entry. For the woman who has difficulty understanding the readings there are no familiar routes. As she enters the unknown it is sug-gested she notice her reactions. The language takes her into herself, evokes a response, in this instance, resistance. What does this tell her of herself? Where does the resistance lead her, rather than what is the fixed meaning of the text (experience)? She begins to pay attention to her own experience, her own feeling. (Denton, pp. 32–33, 1989)

Movement as Sacrifice

The gestural posture of contraction is one of holding. The body tightens in response to an experience—it holds the feeling in its grasp—closing like a fist. In this holding, there is no movement, only the contraction of con-sciousness, the contraction of the heart. Here experience is the ungiven. What would it look like to gesture differently? I am reminded of notions of sacrifice—"an act of offering to deity something precious." The sacrifice is a letting go, a giving back of experience. Utpaladeva, a tenth-century mys-tic, writes, "I bow to him who,/ Drawing the outside world into his heart,/ Worships you, O Lord" (Utpaladeva qtd. in Bailly, 1987, p. 85). I notice that at times in an intensity of experience the heart seems to burn with feeling. Could this be the gift of experience—that it returns us to feeling—the inner flame of the heart? Is it experience that feeds the flame? The notion of for-giveness can be linked to this surrendering of experience. As we for/give we allow a giving back of our frailties, our mistakes—all surrendered to this inner flame. In this gesture there can be no holding of experience. The places of our mistakes "require surrender and letting go: when we let our-selves become vulnerable new things can be born in us" (Kornfield, 1993, p. 79). In this vision the heart's flame is an altar—a sacred site of offering and all experience is simply food for the flame. Relaxing into experience we let go of the places of our own holding. The fist unfolds, finger by finger.

Narratives of Expansion

Today I want the solitude of darkness in my classroom. I dim the lights. The room falls silent. Students sprawl in chairs and on the floor. One small lamp offers interludes of shadow. We breathe in the darkness, the stillness. I can feel twenty bodies filling as one—drenched in silence. After some time my voice stirs the room, gently inviting a return to light, thought, and other.

Always fundamental to my own pedagogy of the heart is the use of meditative and contemplative practice. I integrate three related approaches embodying practices of feeling. The first I identify as an unintentional practice—woundings of the heart that erupt in our human experience—moments of loss, rejection, trauma, physical and emotional pain. These have a profound effect on our consciousness—shifting our psychological boundaries. The wound awakens us to experience. Flames of feeling melt and open the constricted places of the heart. In a meditation practice I invite students to return to a memory of wounding. In this practice we learn the difficult art of staying with the wound—staying with an intensity of feeling. This intensity of feeling has the effect of pulling students into the moment. The emotion acts as a magnet drawing their attention. In various spiritual traditions, the initiate must encounter severe physical trauma, a wounding of the body and psyche, to access an expanded consciousness. Meister Eckhart writes, "The shell must be broken and what is contained in it must come out; for if you want the kernel, you must break the shell" (Eckhart, 1957, p. 237). I am reminded of the hardening surface of the pillow—the contractions that form the shell or crusting of the ego—on the surface of consciousness—the defenses of consciousness. In the midst of the wound, as we invite in comfort, compassion, the gentleness of the heart, old scars soften, places of tightening in the body ease.

Two further methods I use are what I describe as intentional practices. The first of these I refer to as a practice of relaxing into the heart, which cultivates a willingness to stay with experience, to recognize and listen attentively to feeling. As noted earlier it is the tendency to judge an experience which contracts and tightens the heart—that closes her doors. With compassion we begin to relax into experience, into feeling. In facilitating this process I am reminded to hold the image/feeling/experience large—not to constrain it with judgment. Let it be what it needs to be; listen to its message—the sensations and feeling tone of the experience.

A student of mine has great difficulty when we move into meditative states. Relaxing into the breath, into the body, precipitates a heightened state of anxiety. Her body trembles and tightens. I invite her to open her eyes. We stay with the anxiety. As she relaxes into this feeling she describes an emerging image—gentle hands wrapping her body in a velvet cloak. The touch of fabric is soft against her skin and brings a gentle warmth. With the emergence of this image her anxiety subsides. During subsequent meditations she sits, with eyes open, feeling herself wrapped in the soft folds of this cloak. This becomes her practice.

The second of the intentional methods involves conscious practice of filling the heart—learning to nourish the self in thought, feeling, and action. I dramatize this with a glass of water and a drop of red dye. Within seconds of immersion, the water turns red. Similarly, drops of thought, feeling and action color our consciousness. Inviting this notion of filling the heart into the classroom, I suggest that students reflect on what nourishes, what gives pleasure to the self. Here aesthetic experience has much to offer. Dyczkowski (1987) notes that the pleasure we derive from aesthetic experience is "the repose we enjoy when the activity of the mind is momentarily arrested and delights one-pointedly in the source of pleasure. All pleasure, in other words, is essentially spiritual" (p. 147). This juxtaposition of pleasure and the spiritual is unfamiliar. What does it mean to invite pleasure into the body as spiritual practice? States of hate, jealousy, fear, judgment, serve to contract consciousness—to limit and restrain the self. What do states of pleasure offer? I encourage students to explore this— to invite in new qualities—feelings that nourish. With breath and imagination we begin to embody these alternate states.

Sometimes we imagine someone or something loved. As sensations of love, feelings of warmth and openness stream into the body and our awareness, we let go of the memory and stay with this essential feeling. For students who have difficulty experiencing compassion for self, this offers an easier transitional experience. Integrating the breath, we sometimes expand the exercise and imagine breathing these feelings into the body. With each exhalation the feeling expands throughout the body. Soon we are enveloped in feelings of compassion.

Conclusion

I am always putting out fires it seems. Calming the multiple voices—conflicts in the department, between students, with students. A hundred e-mails. Succumbing to institutional life. Playing the game. Applying for grants, for more technology, less human contact. I am always moving away from something—something real. What space for the heart is here?

Recently at a conference on Spirituality and Education in a California mountain retreat, I was inspired by a dialogue with other educators. Three of us gathered under a tree in the woods. Our conversation was animated. My colleague said, "We want our actions to be sustainable." This inspired my own questions: What is sustaining—for me, for our relationships, our community, our earth? How do we create sustaining relationships in the classroom? What sustains the heart?

Later, as I walk in the silence of the forest I hear, "Sustainable action is the heart that moves." The heart that moves is a heart responsive to experience, responsive to the touch of experience. It is a heart able to respond. The heart that is inert like a stone is a heart that does not move; that does not feel the touch of experience—that is not moved by experience. It is a heart that makes no answer to experience. This is the anaesthetized heart, the heart that has no reaction to what it faces. It turns "the sensuous face of the world into monotony, sameness, oneness" (Hillman, 1981, p. 41). So much of our institutional life reinforces monotony and sameness. Our students come to us anxious, inattentive, disengaged. Their minds are arraigned and organized, but their hearts are left off the syllabus. In the curriculum of quiet things, of breath and silence, meditation and narration, they may find a place for the heart.

It is in the light of the heart that we as educators may find the wisdom of compassionate action. Resisting institutional dogma and authority, we must listen to our own hearts, the quiet, still calling of the heart that brings us to the textured moments of experience in stillness, sensation, eros, and suffering. Engaging practices of the heart—relaxing into feeling, filling the heart—we presence a pedagogy of feeling that restores the human contours of experience to institutional life. As we gather images and stories that speak to our own pedagogical tales of the heart we create communities of engagement that sustain and inspire our journeying.

References

Bailly, C. R. (1987). *Shaiva devotional songs of kashmir: A translation and study of Utpaladeva's shivastotravali.* Albany, NY: State University of New York Press.

Denton, D. (1989). *Presence.* Unpublished master's thesis. University of Toronto, Toronto, Ontario, Canada.

Denton, D. (1998). *In the tenderness of stone: Liberating consciousness through the awakening of the heart.* Pittsburgh: Sterling House.

Dyczkowski, M. S. G. (1987). *The doctrine of vibration: An analysis of the doctrines and practices of kashmir shaivism.* Albany, NY: State University of New York Press.

Eckhart, M. (1957). *Meister Eckhart: An introduction to the study of his works, with an anthology of his sermons,* ed. J. Clark. London: Nelson & Sons.

Feuerstein, G. (1990). *Holy madness.* New York: Arkana.

Hillman, J. (1981). *Eranos lectures: The thought of the heart.* Dallas, TX: Spring Publications.

Kornfield, J. (1993). *A path with heart.* New York: Bantam Books.

Muller-Ortega, P. (1989). *The triadic heart of siva: Kaula tantricism of Abhinavagupta in the non-dual shaivism of kashmir.* Albany, NY: State University of New York Press.

Singh, J. (Trans). (1980). *Spanda karikas.* Delhi: Motilal Banarsidass Indological Publishers and Booksellers.

Singh, J. (Trans). (1990). *The doctrine of recognition: A translation of pratyabhijnahrdayam.* Albany, NY: State University of New York Press.

Spirited Teaching

A Pedagogy of Courage

*Communication with the other can be transcendent only as a dangerous life,
a fine risk to be run.*
. —*Emmanuel Levinas (1981, p. 120)*

. . . and from the door in the heavens souls came down pure.
—*Socrates (Republic, Book X, 614D)*

*Love takes off the masks that we fear we cannot live without and know we
cannot live within.*
—*James Baldwin (1962, p. 95)*

Learning to Teach

Every human encounter entails risk. As I face a human Other, I am con-
fronted with the possibility that one of us will not be accepted, that one or
both of us will be hurt, that misunderstandings and failures to communicate will overshadow other possibilities. We may even face the possibility
of hatred. We never really know in advance how any given contact will
turn out. Danger always lurks in the shadows of encounter. Surely, if the

---

Although I titled the sections of this chapter *Learning to Teach* and *Teaching to Learn*
without having prior knowledge of it, thanks to series editor Peter Laurence for refer-
ring me to Anne French Dalke's book, *Teaching to Learn/Learning to Teach: Meditations on the Classroom*, which was written for the series *Studies in Education and Spirituality*. I recommend the book to all who are enthralled by the magic of teaching.

encounter goes beyond the merely social—if it becomes personal—neither of us will emerge unscathed. Such is the dangerous life of a communicator.

The lives of teachers and students are doubly dangerous. When learning and teaching with heart, we run the risk of stirring souls, of shaking each other up, of calling into question the very foundations of existence! When we enter the realm of spirit in teaching and learning, we are tapping into a deep well of anxiety; faith is called into question; despair itself can emerge.

In heartful, spirited education, we are filled with questions—filled to bursting, our pulses pounding. On any given night, we may find ourselves dreaming in the dark, awakening with a shiver.

However, there are two sides to any danger. The philosopher Emmanuel Levinas (1981) writes of the demand—an invocation—to an ethical relation that issues from the face of the human Other. Drawing upon ancient Jewish mystical traditions, Levinas sees encounter with an Other as the ignition of a Holy, limitless light—a light that calls us out into the open, lays us bare, burns in us, and opens us to possibility.

The teacher is the one who leads us into this light. Like a few fortunate denizens of Plato's cave, unbound from our shackles, we, the students, are drawn out into the light. On a good day, we find ourselves dancing in the light. What is the key that releases the shackles? At the center of the true teacher's life is the human welcome, that truly hospitable greeting of the Other wherein our masks are stripped away, and we are laid bare, open to genuine human knowing, to love. If we think of human encounter as an opening to possibility that occurs in the welcoming of the Other into the space and time we co-inhabit, we find that the fine risk, the danger braved, is an open road to joy. Dancing in the light. . .

A teacher is an opener of doors. Hermes, the messenger-god, was also said to be the one assigned the task of leading souls across the threshold from the world of the living to the realm of the dead. Hermeneutic motion is a guiding motion.

Look closely at that great teacher of yours. I'll bet she has wings on her feet.

If we consider the activities of teaching and learning as hermeneutic action, as opening doors of possibility and deliberately running risks, as a dangerous-transcendent life . . . if we think of teaching and learning as firing the sparks that light the kiln in which we solidify the courage to create (May, 1972). . .there may be hope in this Age of Anxiety we now inhabit (Poulos, 2002).

Indeed, there is a place for heartful, courageous action in the academy. For in this spirited approach to pedagogy, an encounter with an Other is not an end, but a beginning—an opening—to reconfiguring living as teaching and learning, and teaching and learning as a welcome and a sharing of gifts. The primary gifts of human life, it turns out, are gifts of the *coeur*—the heart. Teachers who teach from the heart are bound by a pedagogy of the heart-gift (Fr. *coeur*-age: to have heart!).

Pedagogy of heart, pedagogy of courage . . . What follows is a story of risk and gift, of teaching as courage, of learning and teaching as acts of courage, of dreaming in the dark and dancing in the light.

October 1, 1978

Last night I dreamed I was on trial. For the life of me, I could not figure out what I had done. But there I was, in the courtroom, sweating profusely, as the prosecutor made his case. I did not understand a word he said. I looked up at the jury, who were my classmates in Philosophy 101. They laughed derisively, loudly, at me. I opened my mouth to speak, and they laughed even louder. Finally, I yelled, at the top of my lungs, "Know thyself!" The room fell silent.

Then I woke up, a chill running through me, a bit clammy from the sweat dripping off my brow. One of the hazards of studying philosophy at the age of twenty . . .

You see, we have just finished reading Plato's story of the trial of his teacher, Socrates. In my dreams, I have been transformed. I am Socrates. One of the hazards of studying philosophy . . .

Today is my birthday. I am twenty years old. I sit in class, a bit restless, thinking I could be doing other things on this day. The man at the front of the room rants—there is no other word for it—about how young people today do not live up to the simple standard of virtuous curiosity that the Greek youth of 2000 years ago practiced. As I know that most of my classmates have not read the text in preparation for the day, it occurs to me that he has a point.

"Maybe you are right," the professor says suddenly. "Maybe reading this stuff is a waste of time." I sit up a bit, wondering where this is heading. He stares at us. Glares, in fact. Suddenly, I hear my own voice. I blurt out, without thinking, "Wait! That can't be right. I'm dreaming about this stuff." My classmates look at me as though I am now certifiably insane. The teacher pauses, turns to look at me, says softly, "Well . . . tell us your dream . . ."

As the conversation unfolds, and we come to the Delphic injunction, "Know thyself!" The teacher says, "Isn't that precisely Socrates' message to Athens in *The Apology*?"

Yes, I find myself thinking. He took a stand. And for taking that radical stand, he was put to death. One of the hazards of studying philosophy . . . of teaching philosophy . . .

"*Philo* (love) + *Sophia* (wisdom) = philosophy—the love of wisdom. For that, Socrates was put to death. For being a teacher, for corrupting the youth, he was executed," my professor proclaims.

And at that moment, I sit bolt upright in my chair, certain of one thing and one thing only. Like a thunderbolt, a moment of foreknowledge has been given me: Someday, I will be a teacher.

October 1, 1981

Now 23, I still study philosophy, but these days my dreams are even more Kafkaesque. One of the hazards . . .

I dream that I am in a Paris café. At the table next to me is Jean-Paul Sartre. He puffs laconically on a hand-rolled cigarette, glances my way, and notices I am staring at him. So he looks me in the eye, holds me with his gaze, and says, "Hell is other people. And you, *mon ami,* are the fiery center of hell."

I sit bolt upright in bed. There will be no more sleep this night. *Being and Nothingness* is on my bedside table. One of the hazards of studying philosophy . . .

For this malady I suffer, for dreaming dreams about philosophy and philosophers, for questioning my identity, for wondering if, in fact, I am the fiery center of hell, I know where to assign blame. It is these damn teachers—the ones who shake me up, call me out, pull me in, draw the truth out of me, force me to ask, push me to wonder, eat my lunch. It is these damn teachers, the ones who teach with questions not answers, who call my world into question, who force me to struggle, yet nurture me in my unfolding. It is these damn teachers who teach courageously, from the heart. I blame them!

The next day, in my Sartre class, I look at my teacher, Hazel Barnes, the very translator of *Being and Nothingness,* and I understand the lines in her face. It is clear to me that she has suffered the agony of dreaming Sartre, in French.

No wonder her voice is so strong, I think, as she explains the concept of "bad faith." She has felt the betrayal of someone who lives in bad faith. How else to explain the pulse of her voice, the pain and the passion as she speaks? She teaches, and the very blood of her heart flows into words in the air . . .

November 16, 1981

"The Tragic Sense". . . the course title is fitting, as I, with an ever-growing bent toward the dramatic, cultivate a sense of my own tragic life situation. For it is tragic, indeed, to live with the question "Why am I here?"

Our teacher, Nancy, shepherds us through many tragic texts, holding us in a fine balance as we walk that razor's edge of life, the narrow ridge (Buber, 1965) between tragedy and comedy, between catharsis and despair.

We have to do a "creative project" for the course. I suffer, grappling hard with fear, as I choose to perform a monologue from a play. I decide to try the character Harry Hope, the raging alcoholic from Eugene O'Neill's brilliant tragic play, *The Iceman Cometh*.

I practice and practice. Dressed in the local Goodwill Thrift Store's version of a 1930s suit and fedora, I shout the lines into the emptiness of my apartment. I have been studying Stanislavski's "method," wherein the actor tries to access some deep emotional memory in order to really live the character's emotional life. In this case, I am desperately seeking despair.

The day of my performance dawns, and I find I am frozen in terror. I can barely down my morning coffee.

What will I do? I want to bolt away, drop out of school, surrender to the fear. I cannot do this. I cannot.

I sink into a chair. I sit for a long time, literally frozen, paralyzed. I am not even sure I can walk. The dread is just too strong. Slowly a new feeling begins to mingle with the dread. Could it be—despair? Oh, what am I to do? With a mighty effort, I drag myself to my feet, get dressed in my costume, and make my way to class.

It is time. I stand at the front of the class. My teacher, Nancy, sits in the back. I look to her for a cue, and her eyes meet mine. There is a spark there, a hint of heart. It is just the boost I need. I turn my back on my audience, take a deep breath, turn . . . and I am not me. For a few brief moments, I have transcended my self. I am Harry Hope. I fall into a dark despairing diatribe. As my words trail off into silence, I emerge from the trance, at first dimly aware of my surroundings, uncertain if minutes or hours have passed. My fellow students, and my teacher, are standing, giving me a hearty ovation. I sink into my chair, slightly embarrassed but beaming with pride.

October 1, 1996

It is the second year of my doctoral program in Communication. I sit in a course called, somewhat mildly, unobtrusively even, "Organizational Communication."

I find myself thinking: I have been hoodwinked. This course is only marginally about organizational anything.

After all, the first text we read was Erving Goffman's *Behavior in Public Places.*

The teacher, I think, is a shaman. In the indigenous cultures of North and South America, of Indonesia and Africa and Australia and Asia, of virtually every continent on earth, the shaman is something of a liminal human, a person who dwells on the outskirts, on the threshold between civilization and nature.

The shaman is a translator: "The traditional or tribal shaman, I came to discern, acts as an intermediary between the human community and the larger ecological field, ensuring that there is an appropriate flow of nourishment, not just from the landscape to the human inhabitants, but from the human community back to the local earth" (Abram, 1996, p. 7). This teacher acts as an intermediary—what Peter McLaren (1988) has called a "liminal servant"—one who ushers students across a dangerous threshold between the uncivilized/natural world of ambiguity into a civilized/naturalized world of understanding . . . Surely he is a magician.

Even more magical, more wonderful than I can imagine, is that moment when we, as students, can give back the gift. We are reading a particularly difficult passage, and this time he is confused, in the dark. Together, we lead Roy into the light. The tables have turned. We have taken on the role of the shaman. We are dancing in the light.

Organizational Communication? Our dialogue is about much more than that . . . it is about communicative praxis, about humans gathering to connect, about making meaning. It is about the betwixt and between of learning and communicating, about the liminal threshold where most of life begins to unfold . . . It is about becoming, about being-as-becoming. And more. Much more.

For it is about our heartful engagement with each other, about risking, heartfully, courageously, our very place in this world as we come to know . . . one another. It is about giving . . . and receiving . . . a gift of life, of heart.

Hoodwinked, indeed. Magic. My teacher, Roy, is surely a shaman.

Teaching to Learn

So, what is a good teacher? I have watched my great teachers for many years now. I have been an apprentice.

So, what is it about my teachers? How do I know they teach from the heart? How do I know the risks they have taken? What have they done to lead us across that threshold? Several things, in my experience, make me aware that I am enheartened: We talk; I dream; I shiver and sweat. As the process unfolds, I become a new kind of person. In the heartful classroom, something—an energy, a fire, a light in the darkness—is evoked, provoked, lit, stoked . . . I cannot stand still. I must move; I must change; I must take these texts and these people into account in my life beyond the classroom.

I must dream in the dark. I must dance in the light.

As I look back on my life as a student, as I remember my great teachers, I can only think that they are to blame. They are to blame for my passion for learning. They are to blame for this life I have chosen, this life of toil and struggle . . . and joy. They are to blame. As the memories flood in, I feel how these teachers still, even many years later, even after some of them are dead . . . these teachers . . . break my heart, eat my lunch, steal my dreams, stir me up, call me out, make me laugh, make me cry, work on me, push me, pull my chain . . .

And now, all these years later, I am a teacher. Whom will I stir up today?

As this thought comes to me, a student walks into my office. His fists are clenched. He is shaking with barely concealed rage. I welcome him, invite him to sit, ask him, "So what's wrong?"

He does not sit. Instead, he paces in my office, fairly ranting about what has been unfolding in our course together, a small honors seminar in the history of rhetoric.

Rage, I find myself thinking. Well.

He has been reading signs, some subtle, some rather blatant, that unfold as we encounter our course material, Plato's scathing indictments of the sophists. He is not happy, for he has just realized that he has lived his entire life as a sophist; worse, he has lived his life fully subject to the whims of other sophists. It is not often that a student sees such a thing.

His classmates saw it before he did. Hence the rage. When he speaks in class, he sees the signs of their recognition; they have uncovered his game; he has been indicted as a sophist; he is now on trial. The trial takes the form of rolling eyes, little whispered asides, laughter.

His life is indeed tragic. He does not know what to do. He is thinking of dropping out of school. He is in crisis. Last night, he dreamed that he showed up to class naked. This was, perhaps, the final straw.

I search inside me for something to help him, knowing full well that he is in a dangerous place, but also knowing I cannot stop his crisis.

"It hurts, doesn't it?" I ask softly.

He looks like he has been hit in the face with a board. The color runs out of his cheeks. He is stunned. He just stares at me, his lip beginning to quiver a little at the corner. I am afraid he is going to cry.

After a long silence: "Yes," he whispers, and falls into a chair.

Moments tick by. The silence is heavy.

"Why are you in school?" I ask.

"I thought I was here to get a degree. Maybe I'm just wasting my time," he replies.

I think of my Philosophy 101 teacher, Bob. "Maybe you're right; maybe you are wasting your time. But perhaps there are other reasons to go to school," I reply.

Another long pause.

"I will stay," he says.

Who knows? Maybe someday he will be a teacher.

September 11, 2001

It is 11:00 a.m., just two short hours after the world shook, turned upside down, changed forever. As a teacher, I do not know what to do. Though I am not a person who is usually at a loss for words, today I am speechless. The first moments of standing before my class that day are agonizing. I honestly do not know what to do.

Words eventually come, but they seem, at this moment, to fail utterly. How do you talk about something that is unlike anything in your previous experience? For the first time in my teaching career, teaching seems irrelevant.

What we need is time to gasp.

And time to grieve.

And time to wonder.

And, maybe, time to breathe.

Sometimes, silence is called for.

And yet . . . in this moment, I am called to speak. I look into my students' eyes, and tell them what has happened. Questions fly around the room for a time. But soon our questions fail us.

A student rises, and says, "I think we should go . . . be with our loved ones."

This is wisdom rising. I dismiss class.

At the end of the day, after more hours of shock and failing words and disbelief and television images shared with colleagues and students, I leave campus, engulfed in anxiety.

That day, my teaching life changed forever. No longer do I walk in a shroud of expertise, DOCTOR Poulos, sure of my knowledge. I find myself slipping into and out of the world, wondering. Life itself, in these days of CODE ORANGE, whispers into each day as a nearly ineffable question, hovering on lips that, it sometimes seems, might never speak again.

Why do this? Why teach? What is our purpose here?

One day after the horror, I look in the only place I know to find some kind of spark I can send out into the world.

I look into my heart. And there, deep in my heart, are all my great teachers—Bob, Hazel, Nancy, Roy, Will—smiling up at me.

I know what I must do. The next day, I begin class with a simple question: What has changed?

Our dialogue is solemn, but it drives us. We seek meaning, together. Emotions run high. We probe the possibilities. Questioning is the center, but the center does not hold. We are in a liminal state, betwixt and between. We are in an anxious process, seeking to meet the mystery but also to contain the anxiety. Our pulse is pounding through us.

We are in shock. Dismay, outrage, and fear rule the day. Many of us are numb/ silent/angry/sad. Gradually, amid all these contradictory feelings, a desire to do something to help emerges. As we continue our search, ideas and questions fill the air, but few definitive answers. Still, we know, somewhere deep within us, that we must reach out.

I find myself wondering: "What is a teacher, really? Am I a purveyor of information? Or am I called to lead a community of learners across a dangerous, anxiety-filled threshold?"

After many years as a student and a teacher, I know one thing: Coming to know is an act that requires change, a process that, by its very nature, creates anxiety. It is an act of courage. It is an act that takes a lot of heart.

So I think that to teach from a space of compassion, responsibility, and commitment, to draw my students into the light, I must draw on the deep anxiety we all share. I must help by calling it out into the open, by looking closely at it, by helping it to be a spark-lighting energy.

So, together, we move toward knowing via the energy of anxiety, compassion, and the commitment to share our lives, our thoughts, our feelings, our questions, our desires, our interpretations, our dreams, our questions . . . always questions.

As a learning-questioning community, we move, together, beyond anxiety; we spring into new worlds of relating.

These new ways of relating fade into our dreams.

In these post-9/11 days, my dreams haunt me.

These days, like the courses I teach, my dreams invariably begin with a question.

However, these days, when I awaken, there is a glimmer of light peeking in my window. And I know I will dance again.

The playwright Christopher Fry tells the story of a friend who, under the influence of ether, dreamed that a pair of great hands was turning the pages of a very large book—a book that promised to reveal the meaning of life. The pages were alternately tragic and comic, and it became increasingly clear that the last page of the book would offer the last word on that engrossing question. What, my friends, is the meaning of life? The dreamer grew very excited as the last page was about to be turned, and burst into gales of laughter as the great comic secret was revealed.

I like to think I would have woken up before the page was turned. It seems to me that this life of teaching and learning, of learning to teach and teaching to learn—and the communication that enriches, constructs, enacts, and shrouds it—is more like a turning page than a turned one, more like a question than an answer, more tragicomic than tragic or comic, more both/and than either/or, more an opening door than a closing one, more a commencement than a graduation, more a meeting of hearts than a list of answers.

As the days go by in this post-9/11 world, I find myself engrossed by mystery, engulfed in ambiguity. I live in a largely liminal state, betwixt and between. Even as I see the answers coming, I can feel them slipping away, like a fistful of water, like a wispy fog on a Carolina morning. I live in a state of wonder. As Walker Percy (1961) puts it, "And there I have lived ever since . . . in wonder, wondering day and night, never a moment without wonder . . . and not for five minutes will I be distracted from the wonder . . ." (p. 39).

March 12, 2003

As I lay in bed last night, thinking back on my life as a student and a teacher, and pondering the best moments of learning and teaching I have experienced, I fell into a dream. In my dream, all my great teachers—Bob, Hazel, Nancy, Roy, along with many of their colleagues, all my teacher-friends—are standing at the side of a large classroom. I am their student, again, and they are the Greek chorus in an unfolding comic play—or is it tragic?

The chorus, in perfect harmony, tells a story. It is a story of loss and joy, of anger and peace, of truth and lies, of pain and freedom. I consider the story they tell, with care, trying to decipher it, trying to answer the question: Tragedy? Or Comedy?

And, as the story unfolds, I am swept away. I roll on the floor laughing until my ribs hurt. I sob uncontrollably, barely able to breathe. I sit pensively, wondering. I rail at injustice. I am flabbergasted, unable to speak. I sigh, feeling the weight of the world bearing down on my shoulders. I stand tall, proud of my place in the world. I smile compassionately. I curl my lip ironically. I speak eloquently. Words fail me. I am smart. My God, I am so stupid! A spark of understanding lights up my being. I walk about in a fog. I know just where I am. I am lost. I hate this. I love this. I am angry. I am sad. I am joyous. I am depressed. I hurt, so deeply that I do not think I will survive. I am so buoyant—I could fly! I am choking, suffocating, dying inside. I am alive, electrified, leaping. My heart stops—it is broken. My heart races, thrilled to beat so furiously. Sleep overcomes me. The cold water of life splashes me in the face, shocking me into wakefulness.

I walk the razor's edge . . . I am in between these poles of life, a turning page, walking in wonder . . .

Have you ever dreamed about sex? Have you ever had a dream so vivid that . . .

Good, courageous teaching and learning is, in a sense, like a good dream—or a bad one. Good teaching and learning is so vivid that . . . it carries me into a world, transports and transforms me, brings me to the verge of ec-stasy, pulls me deep into agony, breaks my heart, tickles my fancy, freaks me out, digs at me, itches and irritates me, tears me up, makes me laugh and makes me cry, nags at me, heats me up, cools me down, gnaws at me, pokes at me, splashes me, smiles at me, shakes its fist at me, whispers to me, shouts at me, plays with me, makes me work, cajoles and consoles, lulls me into silence, startles me to wakefulness, carries my soul to new heights . . .

Good teaching and learning is like a good dream—or a bad one. It is . . . magical, mystical, beautiful, painful. It is like a turning page, betwixt and between, hovering on the threshold . . .

When I wake up from a good class session, I might know something, or feel something, or wonder about something.

Whatever happens, once we have engaged in this great tragic/comic work of learning and teaching from the heart, we will never be the same again.

For we inevitably find that we have been dreaming in the dark.

And we have been dancing in the light.

References

Abram, D. (1996). *The spell of the sensuous*. New York, NY: Vintage Books.

Baldwin, J. (1962). *The fire next time*. New York, NY: Vintage Books.

Buber, M. (1965). *Between man and man*. (M. Friedman, Ed; R. G. Smith, Trans.). New York, NY: Macmillan.

Dalke, A. F., et.al. (2002). *Teaching to learn/learning to teach: Meditations on the classroom*. New York, NY: Peter Lang Publishing.

Levinas, E. (1981). *Otherwise than being: Or beyond essence*. (A. Lingis, Trans.). Pittsburgh, PA: Duquesne University Press.

May, R. (1972). *The courage to create*. New York, NY: Bantam Books.

McLaren, Peter. The liminal servant and the ritual roots of critical pedagogy. *Language Arts* 65, no. 2 (1988) 164–179.

Percy, W. (1961). *The moviegoer*. New York: Alfred A. Knopf, Inc.

Plato (1992). *Republic*. (G.M.A. Grube, Trans.). Indianapolis, IN: Hackett Publishing Company, Inc.

Poulos, C. (2002). The death of ordinariness: Living, learning, and relating in the age of anxiety. *Qualitative Inquiry*, Volume 8, No. 3, 288–301.

Contributors

Tony Arduini received his Ph.D. from the Department of Speech Communication at Southern Illinois University-Carbondale in August of 2000 and is currently teaching speech at Kirkwood Community College in Cedar Rapids, IA. He has a range of research interests, including theories of embodiment, instructional communication, communication and critical theory, and interpersonal communication.

Will Ashton is an Assistant Professor of Educational Foundations at Illinois State University, where he teaches courses in education philosophy, leadership ethics, and policy analysis. He holds a doctorate in philosophy of communication from Southern Illinois University (2000). His work has been published widely in journals.

Diana Denton, an Assistant Professor of Drama and Speech Communication at the University of Waterloo teaches courses in leadership, communication and performance. She has a Ph.D. in Holistic and Aesthetic Education from the University of Toronto (1996). Her publications include her book *In the Tenderness of Stone: Liberating Consciousness Through Awakening the Heart* and articles and poems in various journals.

Deanna L. Fassett received her Ph.D. in Speech Communication from Southern Illinois University, Carbondale. She is Assistant Professor of Communication Studies at San Jose State University. She has published essays in several education and communication studies journals, including Communication Education, Multicultural Education, and Qualitative Inquiry. Dr. Fassett is currently working on a new project exploring instructional communication and critical pedagogy.

Robert Hostetter (Ph.D., Northwestern University), is Professor of Communication Arts and Theatre at North Park University in Chicago, where he teaches classes in dramatic literature, dramatic writing, film studies, performance studies, and conflict transformation. He has written eight plays, and conducted three oral history projects. His play, *The Longing*, and a video by the same title, are based on oral history stories recorded in Palestine and Israel. He is married and the father of two daughters.

Whitney Hoth has taught at numerous colleges and universities in both the United States and Canada. Currently he is Professor of English and Coordinator of Curriculum Development at Fanshawe College in London, Ontario. He has published articles on technology, literature, and culture.

Andrew Houston is an Assistant Professor in the Department of Drama and Speech Communication at the University of Waterloo. He teaches courses in acting, performance studies and theatre history and specializes in site-specific performances.

Denise A. Menchaca earned her Ph.D. at Southern Illinois University. She is an Assistant Professor in the School of Communication Studies and the Department of Theatre and Film Studies at Bowling Green State University. She is completing a manuscript on the role of the Catholic icon Our Lady of Guadalupe on the socialization processes of Mexican-Americans. She is a performance studies scholar whose research focus is concerned with the writing and performing of identity.

Christopher N. Poulos is Assistant Professor of Communication at the University of North Carolina-Greensboro. An ethnographer and philosopher of communication, he teaches courses in relational communication, dialogue, rhetoric, and film studies. His work has appeared in *Qualitative Inquiry, American Communication Journal, Southern Communication Journal, Cultural Studies*, and in the book *9/11 in American Culture.*

Maria Schmeeckle is an Assistant Professor of Sociology at Illinois State University. She teaches courses about families in society, and enjoys doing service learning projects with her students. In her research, she explores subjective perceptions of family boundaries among today's complex family structures. She plans to publish several articles from this work in the near future. In her spare time, she practices tae kwon do, attends spirituality retreats, and works to promote peace and justice locally and globally.

Peninnah Schram, storyteller, author, and recording artist, is Associate Professor of Speech and Drama at Yeshiva University's Stern College and the Azrieli Graduate School. She is the author of seven books of Jewish folktales, including *Jewish Stories One Generation Tells Another* and *Stories Within Stories: From the Jewish Oral Tradition.* She has recorded a CD, *The Minstrel and the Storyteller: Stories and Songs of the Jewish People,* with singer/guitarist Gerard Edery. As a storyteller, Peninnah is a recipient of the prestigious *Covenant Award for Outstanding Jewish Educator* and the National Storytelling Network's 2003 *Lifetime Achievement Award.* She is the Founding Director of the Jewish Storytelling Center at the 92nd Street Y in New York City.

Celeste N. Snowber, Ph.D. is a dancer, educator, and writer who is an Assistant Professor in the Faculty of Education at Simon Fraser University in Burnaby, British Columbia, Canada. She works in the area of dance education, arts-based educational research, and teacher education. She has authored several books including, *Embodied Prayer* and *In the Womb of God* and has published numerous articles and poetry included in the *Journal of Curriculum Theorizing, Educational Insights, English Quarterly, Teacher Education Quarterly,* and *Qualitative Inquiry.* Celeste continues to integrate modern dance, improvisation, and poetry in her performance and is presently finishing a manuscript, titled, *Ocean Lover,* which explores the natural landscape as a metaphor for spiritual formation. She lives with her three lively boys in Port Moody, British Columbia.

Cathy Toll is a faculty member with the Center for Reading and Literacy at Illinois State University. She teaches graduate courses in theories of literacy, literacy assessment, and curricular change. Her research focuses on school change, the politics of education, and teacher growth. She works extensively with literacy coaches to assist them in supporting growth and change in literacy instruction.

John T. Warren received his Ph.D. in Speech Communication and Performance Studies from Southern Illinois University, Carbondale. He is Assistant Professor of Communication Studies in the School of Communication Studies at Bowling Green State University. He has published essays in several education and communication studies journals, including *Educational Theory, Communication Education,* and *Text and Performance Quarterly.* His book, *Performing Purity: Whiteness, Pedagogy and the Reconstitution of Power* (Peter Lang, 2003). Warren is working on a new project investigating critical performative pedagogy.

Peter L. Laurence &
Victor H. Kazanjian, Jr.
General Editors

Studies in Education and Spirituality presents the reader with the most recent thinking about the role of religion and spirituality in higher education.
It includes a wide variety of perspectives, including students, faculty, administrators, religious life and student life professionals, and representa-
tives of related educational and religious institutions. These are people who
have thought deeply about the topic and share their insights and experiences through this series. These works address the questions: What is the
impact of religious diversity on higher education? What is the potential of
religious pluralism as a strategy to address the dramatic growth of religious
diversity in American colleges and universities? To what extent do institutions of higher learning desire to prepare their students for life and work in
a religiously pluralistic world? What is the role of spirituality at colleges
and   universities,
particularly in relationship to teaching and learning pedagogy, the
cultivation of values, moral and ethical development, and the fostering of
global learning communities and responsible global citizens?

For additional information about this series or for the submission of manu-
scripts, please contact:

> Peter L. Laurence
> 5 Trading Post Lane
> Putnam Valley, NY 10579

To order other books in this series, please contact our Customer Service
Department:

> (800) 770-LANG (within the U.S.)
> (212) 647-7706 (outside the U.S.)
> (212) 647-7707 FAX

Or browse online by series:

> www.peterlangusa.com